You Are THAT!

Volume 1

Sri Ramana Maharshi

Sri H.W.L. Poonja
(Papaji)

YOU ARE THAT!

Volume 1

Satsang with Gangaji

You Are THAT!
Volume 1

© Gangaji 1995

Front cover photo: Walking Sky (Bearheart Neuhaus)
Back cover photo: Isabelle Cozart
Cover design: Jennifer Miles

Printed in the USA on acid-free, recycled paper.

ISBN 0-9632194-3-X
Library of Congress Card Catalog #95-71521

Table of Contents

Blessings and gratitude to all those who transcribed satsang tapes, to Dan Hawthorne for formatting the book and getting it ready for press, to Eli Jaxon-Bear for his inspiration and consultation, to Al Drucker for his invaluable editing suggestions, and especially to Shanti Einolander for enthusiastically and tirelessly entering the numerous changes while contributing to the overall book production.

For Beloved Papaji

Radiant manifestation of Self
whose recognition and confirmation
removed all pretense of doubt.
It is only through his grace that satsang
with Gangaji makes its appearance here
in consciousness.

Formal satsangs are public gatherings, free and open to everyone, in which Gangaji interacts with those asking questions, giving reports, or making comments.

You Are That! contains selected excerpts from satsangs held throughout 1993-1995 in various locations of Northern India, Nepal, Bali, and the Western United States, including Maui, Hawaii.

Throughout these pages, words such as That, the Beloved, It, Self, and Truth are in reference to that vast, unnamable, eternal Presence; sometimes called God, Christ-consciousness, Buddha-mind, existence, awareness, or whatever term used in the vernacular of each particular culture and sub-culture.

Welcome to Satsang

That which you yearn for, that which you hunger for, is That which is always present. That is who you truly are.

When I say *you,* I am not referring to your body. Your body is in that. I am not referring to your thoughts. Your thoughts are in that. I am not referring to your emotions. Your emotions appear in and disappear in that. I am not speaking of your circumstances. Circumstances too appear in and disappear in that.

Bodies, thoughts, emotions, and circumstances change. They appear and disappear. They may be good or bad. They may be pleasing or displeasing. The truth of who you are is permanent and unmoving. The great, good news is that however you might *imagine* yourself, you can recognize who you *truly* are. Regardless of the experience of yourself as a body, or as the thought, *I am this body,* you can receive the direct transmission of truth from your own Self. That transmission is satsang. Satsang confirms your true identity as pure consciousness, free of all perceived constraints.

When this good news is heard, really heard, there is immeasurable opening. No one has ever reported an end to realizing the Self. What does end is the preoccupation with imagining yourself to be some particular entity separate from boundless consciousness.

Self-realization is not something that can be captured in words. Although words will be used, no word that anyone has ever spoken has touched the glory of the true Self. I am here to point you to that, to celebrate that, and to laugh at the very flimsy excuse that something could ever really obstruct that.

I do not have anything to teach you. Self-realization is not about learning. I am not asking you to remember anything. I am not asking you to do anything or to get anything new. Nothing new is needed. I am asking you to realize you are already that which you want. And I am simply suggesting, as my teacher suggested to me, and as his teacher suggested to him, that you take one instant, one millisecond to allow the activity of the mind to stop.

In that millisecond, what a discovery is made! In that millisecond, you receive the invitation to surrender to what is revealed when there is no attention on body, thought, emotion, or circumstance. This is a momentous instant! In this instant the body is gone. In this instant of perfect silence you discover what is permanently here, what has always been here, what is permanently you. This instant of silence is the invitation to true refuge, true retreat, true peace, regardless of comings and goings.

What an instant this is! In this instant there is no dwelling on the past, there is no speculating on the future, and there is no analyzing the present in relation to the past or the future. In this instant there is no mental preoccupation, there is no conditioned existence. There is only that pure, pristine consciousness. In this instant you are in satsang.

Somehow, by some stroke of good luck, your individual consciousness has been called to satsang. You have heard the words that you are Truth itself. Now you are free to discover yourself as Truth. You are free to rest in that Truth.

You are free to be happy, regardless of bodies, thoughts, emotions, or circumstances. You are free to be who you truly are.

Welcome to satsang.

The Only True Desire

True desire is desire for reunion with God, desire for Truth, desire for an end to suffering. This true desire is the core of all other distorted and misplaced desires.

If passion for Truth is not recognized, then all the distorted imitations of true passion— all the other usual passions of greed, hate, lust, envy— arise and lead to suffering.

Be honest with yourself. Ruthlessly honest. Ask yourself, "What do I want?"

Do you want to be free?

Do you really want to realize Truth?

If you just want a nice spiritual high sometimes, you are welcome to it of course. That is somewhat like putting your toe into the ocean. It feels very good, and the ocean doesn't mind if you just put your toe in. Yet, there is the possibility of diving into the ocean of Truth totally with no hope of re-emerging. Dive and see.

• • •

I've heard you say, put all of your desires into the one desire for freedom.

Yes, that's right. Freedom is the true desire.

Well, what do I do with that?

What do you "do" with it?

1

Do I act on it or what?

If you put all of your desires into this one desire, *it* does with *you*, totally. Freedom is vast. It is impossible for you to do anything with it.

Who you imagine yourself to be is annihilated by the revelation of freedom. You, as you have known yourself to be, are no more. You, as you have imagined yourself to be, are revealed to be non-existent. There remains only That.

Don't imagine that you will do something with freedom. This idea is the arrogance of egocentric mind. You will be enfolded in such an embrace that there is no thought of *you* left. Freedom is nothing that can be "done with." "Doing with" has to do with everything else. The power of mind can appear to do something with something. However, in true realization, all of the power of mind is consumed by the source of mind.

Divine consummation is the feast of the Divine on its soul.

Surrender! Let yourself be eaten by God however God pleases.

• • •

Sometimes I feel like that desire just burns inside, and I want to bring it into the everyday reality.

Give up the idea that your insatiable thirst and search for truth are separate from everyday reality. Relative reality appears in absolute reality. Everyday reality cannot be separate from the absolute.

There is no everyday life without truth. There is no appearance of any phenomenon without truth. All belongs to truth.

If you have the desire to realize the flame of truth, and you imagine that you can somehow put the flame aside until your life is convenient, you are tricking yourself with postponement, tricking yourself by keeping the illusion of separation active.

I go back and forth between external searching and going within. I feel I need something outside myself.

Okay, fine. I too said, "I need something outside myself. I am not able to do it on my own. I intellectually know it's all within, but I'm not experiencing it." So I met my guru. He appeared to be outside myself while saying, "I am within you!" This appearance occurred in my everyday life. Do you get the import of this?

If you have insatiable thirst for truth, finally you will discover distinctions of outside and inside to be inaccurate. There is no outside separate from inside. These boundaries are mental boundaries. Boundaries that appear to be real and are thought to be real, but in truth, are not real.

I am on the apparent outside pointing to that which is both here in myself and here in you. That which is in every moment of your life. You will not find truth someplace else, and then bring it back into your life. It is already present.

If you really have a thirst, you will see it everywhere, because it is all you will be looking for.

I want to be slain by your power. Please slay me.

Your concepts are being slain.

Die to everything you have ever known about who you are. Die to the habit of following any thought that defines who you are.

If you don't follow thought, it can't stick anywhere, it can't continue. Realize what remains when there is no thought. This that remains has no need of a thought to be. This that *is*, before and after all thought, has no use for the terms "inside" or "outside."

I don't use special magic here. If I did, then satsang would be simply an exchange of trances. Maybe you would feel good, and maybe there would be kundalini* moving, but personal identification would remain intact. Reality is much more simple. There is no need of special magic if what you are searching for is permanent and eternal truth, located everywhere, in everything, with no possibility of being excluded from everyday life.

The truth is that no one can slay you. You can be invited into annihilation, or into the ocean, or into satsang. By accepting that invitation, you discover you are beyond annihilation— only ideas of who you are can be annihilated. By accepting the invitation, you realize you are the one who offers the invitation.

Is it time to accept your Self? You have free choice.

You are free to continue your personal trance. You are free to suffer, and you are free to put suffering behind you.

---

*   kundalini - Extraordinary movement of energy within the body.

This is a moment of reckoning. Do not take this moment casually or trivially. Recognize that for whatever reason, you are aware of the possibility of realizing the truth of yourself as limitless consciousness. This possibility has somehow penetrated your conditioned personal existence. What good luck!

• • •

The habit of thinking is very strong. The pain and suffering are so very strong that nothing seems to penetrate.

Ask yourself, "What do I want? What do I *really* want?"

There's still a lot of wanting things to come out right.

When you say, "I want to end the suffering, and I know how the suffering should be ended. . .it will be ended if certain things turn out a certain way," the habit of mind is fed. This statement insures the habit of thinking and discussing.

When I say "thinking," I am not speaking of fresh insights. I am speaking of those same old thoughts that are thought and re-thought over and over and are unnecessary mental agitation.

Who you are is wisdom itself, and wisdom is not found in obsessive thinking. You are intelligence itself. You are clarity itself. Relax and allow that to reveal itself. Allow clarity to surprisingly reveal itself, with no thought of how it should reveal itself, or what the revelation will be when it does reveal itself.

Obviously you are free to continue the habit of commentary. You are free to discuss forever. The power of mind is a toy, and you are free to continue with it or to put it aside. In putting the habit aside, see what hasn't been played with, what hasn't been touched, what has never moved.

You are always free to pick up the mind and begin the play again. If you don't overlook for a moment that which is before, during, and after all mind activity, unnecessary suffering is finished.

• • •

There may be enormous pain in any individual life. Pain is part of the texture of life. It is the unnecessary suffering that habits of mind support. When pain is met as it is, as simply pain, it can even be experienced as beautiful. It doesn't need to be anything different. When it is rejected and something "not painful" is reached for, pain is experienced as suffering.

The true spiritual quest is not necessarily comfortable. Many people begin the spiritual quest searching for comfort. However you begin it, what is finally revealed is depth of being that leaves all notions of comfort and discomfort behind.

True joy includes both happiness and unhappiness. Recognize that, and you are no longer bound by grasping for pleasure and rejecting pain. True joy embraces all polarities, all action and inaction.

There comes a time to examine one's life with ruthless honesty. Has true, deep desire really been touched by accumulation of objects— physical, mental, or emotional?

Speaking the truth is opening to the recognition that true fulfillment has nothing to do with circumstances. In the willingness for circumstances to be as they are, in that moment of stillness, there is a great recognition of that which is untouched by any circumstance.

In that moment of humility, the arrogance of "I know what it is I need to make me happy" is unmasked. Arrogance unmasked has no power. Recognize what has always been present, waiting to be seen.

What I am saying is very simple. I am saying you are already free. Who you are has always been awake. You have just been playing a game with yourself, and since you are who you are, this game is quite intense. For a moment, put the game aside.

I am not asking you to remember who you are. I am asking you to put everything aside and discover what has never really been forgotten. See what has always been present. Then this love affair, this true love can reveal itself.

Self-love is not self-love as in liking the body or liking the personality. I am not speaking of the body or the personality. The body may be beautiful or ugly. It doesn't matter. In Self-love, what is loved is what is unaffected by evaluations of beauty, ugliness, or personality.

I am speaking of discovering who you truly are. In this discovery, you discover you are in love with that.

• • •

Do you desire things for the future at all, or is it a matter of riding the wave of the moment?

What I desire in this moment and in the future is your awakening. Please, satisfy this desire. (laughter) Then I will leave you alone.

I desire this in past, present, and future. Yes, this desire keeps me reincarnating. I have chosen to reincarnate in this moment only to fulfill this desire. Now, what do you desire?

I desire to express myself.

You cannot truly express yourself until you first discover who you are. Before that discovery, you are just expressing some idea of yourself. Generally, in our culture, expressing yourself means saying what you think and feel. This is expressing thoughts and feelings. Discover who you are, and expression *is* that.

• • •

Is it greed or wisdom to want to be in your presence?

Maybe it is greed for wisdom.

There is nothing wrong with wanting to be in my presence. Through this desire, you may discover who I am. If you discover who I am, then you must in that same instant discover who *you* are. This is what your greed is for, what the yearning is for.

In conditioned existence, divine hunger gets funneled into distorted passions. Then the word "greed" has a nasty connotation, because distorted passions always lead to suffering. In the hunger to realize your Self is found wisdom itself. Then passions are no temptation. They are dull by comparison. To feed the desire for truth reveals fulfillment. Lesser passions are never satisfied.

I welcome your hunger for Self-discovery. It is the desire for the true embrace.

Truth is being evoked in you. That evocation seems to come from me to you. In reality, what is calling for itself is evoking itself. Follow your yearning to its source.

I don't want to remove your hunger. I want to feed it. Make your hunger an all-consuming desire to know your true Self, to live that, to speak that, to give up the choice of any possibility of denying that. Yoke yourself to that.

I welcome you in my presence. I recognize you. I know you to be my own Self. I see that. I confirm that, and I point to the endless revelation of that, in sickness and in health, in pain and in pleasure.

It is through divine grace that satsang has arisen in your consciousness. The invitation is extended to never leave satsang. Leave behind all denial of satsang. Leave behind all denial of the truth you hunger for.

• • •

Do you have any suggestions on how to cultivate more of the desire for liberation?

Honor it. Respect it. Do not trivialize it. Do not make it just another conversational topic. To recognize the truth of who you are is the most sacred, the most precious, the most unimaginable gift.

What a gift of this lifetime, in these times, that somehow true desire is revealed. The opportunity is to foster true desire, to let it live your life, to let it reveal its fulfillment.

What a lucky birth. Don't squander the treasure of your birth.

• • •

I'm feeling some appreciation for the statement I've heard you make, "Need nothing and then see what happens." I could feel the parts of me that would resist even the idea of needing nothing. Then I heard something else coming from the core. You didn't say have nothing. You said NEED nothing.

Well, now I say *have* nothing. Have nothing, need nothing, be nothing. That which has been feared the most— to be nothing, to be nobody, to having nothing at all— be *that*, and see if what you have feared the most does not hold the greatest gem.

• • •

Could you speak about the contradiction between having no desire for the Self, and the sense that there is a "me" here— particularly in regards to work and relationships?

You *are* the Self. Everything is that.

If there is no desire for Self-recognition, there is pre-occupation with "me" and "my" work and "my" relationships and "my" eating and "my" sleeping and "my" acquiring and "my" losing and "my" victories and "my" defeats. All of that is "me" and "my story." Suffering is the general condition of "my story."

In a very rare lifetime there arises a desire for recognition of true Self. When this divine desire appears, satsang appears. Satsang reveals that never, even for a moment, have you not been that true Self.

Satsang is not an invitation to get more for "me." There are many opportunities in the world for that. Satsang is about the ending of the preoccupation with "me-ness."

Mysteriously, in the ending of the personal story, completion and fulfillment are experienced.

If there is no desire for true Self, then it is not time to realize who you really are. Desire for true Self arises somehow— mysteriously, unbidden. Who can say why? It has nothing to do with background, family, culture, race, or prior knowledge. It arises on its own.

• • •

We all know the hell of being tormented by personal desires. Perhaps now you recognize the exquisite torment of true desire which calls you inward, calls you to silence, calls you to surrender all false distorted desire.

You know the desire for more; more wealth, more food, more shelter, more experience. You know that there is never final satisfaction in following these objects of desire. There may be momentary satisfaction, and for that moment there is desirelessness. What peace! What glory!

Because of mistaken identification, this peace is usually attributed to the acquisition of something. Finally there is recognition that desire is never satisfied through acquisition and accumulation of objects. Because of maturity you can finally ask yourself, "What do I really want? What is it I *truly* want?"

You believed that you wanted more things, and you got more things. Then there is a glimmer of understanding that things don't give you what you yearn for. Whether you have more and better things or whether you don't have them, things are secondary.

You believed that you wanted more personal power. Then you wanted more proof of personal power. You acquired proof of personal power, but personal power didn't finally satisfy either. No accumulation of objects has released you from the suffering of desiring.

What is it that you want really, finally, so that with the last breath of your lifetime you can honestly say, "I received what it was I wanted."

I ask you to consider who you are *really*. I promise that if this is deeply considered, your lifetime will not be a wasted lifetime. Your lifetime will not be lived in vain pursuit of false and misdirected desires. It will be lived as a celebration and an invitation. It will not be a lifetime of regret. It will be a lifetime of inspiration. It will be a lifetime that is a beacon.

By recognizing the depth of the answer to the question, "Who am I?" the fire of true identity will spread. It has spread to you.

Let it be revealed in you. Let it spread through you.

Relationship to the Guru

Are you a guru to us?

I am your own Self. I am perceived as whatever you project onto me. You may see sister or mother or friend or guru. Someone even told me once that I was like a big food truck. A letter in satsang yesterday called me the mass murderer of the false self, and of course there are also those who see me as the enemy.

Whatever is projected onto me, I know to be just a projection. I am steady at the present knowing that I am your own Self.

Project whatever you want as long as you hear what I am saying. If you have to call me guru to hear what I am saying, fine. So listen. The guru says, "I am your own Self. I am not separate."

This is what my guru said to me. I needed to hear my guru say it. Some will be able to hear truth from sister, mother, friend, or enemy.

I've tried doing it myself and failed. There seems to be something in you that has stabilized. I was wondering if you feel it's because of having had another person's help?

Before I met my guru, I had tried as much as I knew socially, politically, and spiritually. In each case I found the same basic knot of greed and insecurity, fear and hate. I was not satisfied, and in that dissatisfaction I called out for help.

13

What happened in the relationship between you and your guru?

First, I saw something in him that I had not seen before: something enormous and deep in a welcoming, down-to-earth, human form. In that meeting with him, I recognized something other than what my previous experience, desires, agenda, and planning had revealed.

I recognized that our meeting had mysteriously come from my cry for help. When I had prayed for help, I knew that I didn't know if enlightenment was real. Maybe it was just a story told to give hope so we could be a little happier. If it was not real, I wanted to know that too. I wanted to know what is true.

I recognized that the meeting with my guru had somehow manifested out of that prayer, so I paid close attention.

He literally grabbed me and shook me and said: "Don't miss this opportunity!" It was a shock, like a slap and an embrace at the same time. In an exquisite embrace, what has never been experienced before is experienced, and a different dimension of possibility comes into awareness.

Papaji said, "Stop! Put down every strategy. Put away everything you have ever learned. Forget every technique. Be absolutely still."

I listened to him.

I really can't say what I experienced in that moment. I have tried many times. Whatever I say is still not what I experienced. Whatever I say creates a limited image. I only can call it grace.

I wrote him a letter today saying:

"First your grace reveals understanding.
Then your grace reveals experience.
Then your grace reveals realization.
In realization, experience and understanding can
come and go.
Realization is realizing what has always been."

In realization, what is realized is that which has always
been stable. Then yes, *this* is stability.
Lastly I said:

"Finally, your grace reveals itself as all of life."

All of life, with nothing excluded. Not just the good part
of life, but all of life.

• • •

*You say that a true teacher will point you to your true Self.
Do you mean in any tradition whether it is Hindu, Christian,
Buddhist, etc.?*

Yes. The foundation of all religions is the mysterious,
unknowable, ecstatic union with the Divine. What gets
built out of that foundation is a structure of tradition, a
path, a way to get there.

There are people within all traditions who have been os-
tracized or even burned or beheaded because they have
broken through the structure to arrive at union. When the
tradition becomes the barrier, it must be broken through,
regardless of consequences.

15

So the vehicle really isn't as important as arriving at that realization?

The vehicle, if it is the living truth, *is* the arriving at that realization. It is the recognition of your own Self.

Christ said, "I and my Father are one." This recognition is that the vehicle, the teacher, the Father, the Mother, is none other than your own Self. Not metaphorically, but actually and literally. Your own Self *appearing* in different forms, but realized as same Self.

There are countless teachers: known and unknown, human and inhuman, physical, mental, emotional, and astral. However, the satguru* is the teacher that points to the absolute end of the suffering of separation. The satguru points so clearly and with such strength, that it is realized to be your own Self pointing to itself.

How can I know that the teacher is indeed the teacher you speak of?

You know.

Your knowing has nothing to do with what anyone else says.

You are very lucky if you recognize your teacher right away, but instant recognition is not necessary.

There is nothing wrong with initial doubt and taking the time to check out an attraction. Ultimately you know. Then the challenge is to surrender. The challenge is to

---

*   satguru - The true teacher; recognized as not separate from one's own Self.

honor what you know beyond knowing, and to accept the knowing beyond any attempt to mentally prove.

Ultimately you must trust yourself. Some people fear to trust and think, "Yes, I've made that mistake. I trusted myself and ended up losing all my money, or job, or position." *Really* trusting yourself takes no accounting of what appears to be lost in trusting. I am directing you to trust the deepest intuitive knowing within you, regardless of the inconvenience.

You might begin with relative trust, but if you honor the trust you have, if you follow it, and if you are willing to be both uncomfortable and open, then relative trust can take you to absolute trust.

People might say they want a teacher, but often what they really want is some powerful person to do what *they* want done. When these people pray to God that *thy* will be done, what is really meant is, "*My* will be done."

When you get into relationship with your Self as teacher, it is usually quite ruthless. There is no possibility to own, or control, or direct.

Many people go to Lucknow* to meet Papaji, and most see how astounding it is that this man is love itself. He wants nothing from anyone except their own happiness, and at whatever level happiness is wanted, he will meet that. He wants you to be happy. How could he not? He is your own Self.

People who really look deeper get to experience the endless depth of a raging tiger who will destroy your suf-

---

*   Lucknow - City in Uttar Pradesh, India where H.W.L. Poonja resides and holds satsang.

fering blessedly and ruthlessly. He is *absolutely* loving. Still wanting nothing from you, he will search out the last little corner of hidden identification with the ego and rip it out by the heart.

This is what I call a teacher. Anything else is just child's play . . . playing a game of awakening, while always attempting to maintain control.

• • •

Isn't there a danger of getting attached to a master?

The danger is in getting detached from the master. There will be many temptations to attempt to detach yourself. Becoming attached is the good luck.

This question arises primarily for Westerners. In the West ,we have a strong idea of independence. In the East, the strong idea is of dependence. Both of these ideas are just concepts, still within the realm of the mind.

If you have met a true master, you will find it is impossible to adopt either stance. You are not allowed to imagine yourself as either dependent, or independent.

The true master is first found in your core. This is the satguru. The true teacher exists within the core of all being. In the core of your being is something stronger and deeper than any thought or emotion, and this something must be followed.

It is essential to recognize the master which is alive within you. Nothing is possible before that. Before that recognition, you remain at the whim of society, culture, family, and all other conditioning agents. If the meeting with the master within is a strong, true meeting, there is the recognition that regardless of what happens, you must follow that. If you lose your reputation, you must follow that. If you lose your status, your family, even your happiness, you must follow that. At the risk of losing your life, you follow that.

When a physical manifestation of that internal meeting is needed, it appears. If you recognize your satguru in external form, you are very lucky. Your luck is a measure of your surrender to the master within. Then the more challenging surrender, the heart surrender, begins.

I never planned on having a guru. How could I have imagined such luck? I could not have. I came out of a particular culture, and I imagined my teacher to be somewhat like a guardian angel. I wanted my angel to just hold me and rock me. Of course, when I met my master, he did hold me and rock me in the embrace of Truth.

The holding and rocking is the initial meeting. Then the master reveals itself to be not separate from life itself. Life does not always hold you and rock you. Life slams you against the wall. Life gives you everything, and then life takes everything back. A true master is as relentless as life itself. In the relationship with life, with guru, you are tempted to run away. Do not run. Do not attempt to become unattached.

In the initial embrace, recognize what can never be taken away.

Once Papaji said to me, "If God itself comes down and says to you, 'You are not free, you are not realized,' then turn your back."

God Itself may come down and say, "No, not you," and in your surrender to the satguru, you realize that this too is only the working of the conditioned mind.

When I speak of surrendering to the guru, I am not suggesting you accept all opinions or beliefs or preferences that may arise in the guru's mind. To surrender to the guru is to steadfastly surrender to the truth the guru reveals. The particular form through which it makes itself thoroughly known to you (in my case Papaji) is to be treasured and honored as the embodiment of that which is revealed.

Be attached in love, as you are eternally attached in reality.

• • •

When someone described what they experienced after you left last night, you said, "Well, then don't let me leave." It shook me because I had let you leave too, and I realized if I let you leave, I let myself leave. It's all the same thing.

You imagined that I left. Leaving is only in the imagination. Me leaving, you leaving– it is all imagination.

Then I must have been aware of my imaginings, instead of who I am.

Yes, isn't that the condition? It is believed that what is seen with the eyes is reality. The conviction is that what is felt through the senses is reality. As you know, what you see and feel changes. All of that changes in *you*. You are the constant. In either limited awareness or unlimited awareness, awareness is always present, and awareness is who you are.

I won't let you leave anymore.

I could never possibly go anywhere.

What a relief, isn't it? We are deeply conditioned by the belief in appearance as reality. Suffering arises from the belief in apparent separateness, and apparent comings and goings. So deep is the conditioning that apparent leavings play an important part in true spiritual understanding.

After I had met and been with Papaji, and it was time to return to the states, I went to his home at 7:00 in the morning and said, "I can't leave. There is no way I can go."

He said, "That's right. There is no possible way you can go."

I knew there was nothing else I could say to him in that moment, and I also knew that I was definitely going to experience getting on the plane later in the day. It was quite clear that some experience of staying rather than going was not what he was pointing me toward.

For a time after I returned to the states, I experienced intense longing with a strong tendency to run from that longing. I felt that I had to go back to India where he was.

Through grace I stopped my attempts to return to someplace, and instead I dove directly into the longing. In the direct experience of longing, I realized, *I have not gone! My guru is here! The truth of my guru's being and the truth of my being is the same. Same being!*

• • •

What is this magic chemistry of being with someone who is teaching you? There is such a special energy.

Yes, absolutely special. You are with someone who does not believe for a moment that you are separate, regardless of appearance, feelings, thoughts, attraction, or repulsion. This is nectar. It is what you know in your heart of hearts to be true. Being with someone in this special way is satsang.

Will it jump from you to me, or do I have to work for it?

It is contagious! You don't have to work for it. What you have to do is listen, and that doesn't mean that you listen when you are in formal satsang and then stop listening when you walk out the door. Listen twenty-four hours a day, and from that, true hearing happens quite naturally.

• • •

Could you comment on your experience and/or knowledge of the male teacher and female student relationship, especially when it is sexual?

Whatever the gender combination, it is similar to the relationship of parent and child. In the intimate relationship of student and teacher, it is possible to recognize your spiritual parent and receive the true parenting that had never been offered before.

If our parents had been enlightened, the relationship of teacher and student would not be needed. We have not had enlightened parents. We have had parents who passed on to us what was passed on to them, which was misery and suffering. False aspirations based on attainment, defense of what was attained and grasping for what was not attained, have been our legacy.

The opportunity to receive the transmission of truth is the promise of the teacher and student relationship. It is a precious, rare, secret, subtle relationship, and like the parent and child relationship, it is often misused. Even if the teacher has realized a great deal, emanates shakti* and speaks wisdom, if there is any unburned residue of misery and abuse that was passed on to the teacher by his or her parents– or guru– then the legacy of abuse will continue.

• • •

Tomatoes were once believed to be poisonous until a courageous soul publicly ate one. Then the paper tiger, the lie, was clearly exposed. I have asked you for guidance and help, yet I am unable to fully trust you. My life-long core issue about trust and the inability to discriminate has surfaced, waving its demon banner. Where and how does foolish blind trust meet discrimination? I cannot override the good-sense safety mechanism, so I ask you to show me a tomato or some way through this.

I have shown you a tomato. I have offered you a tomato. I have opened a tomato. I have swallowed a tomato. I have pushed a tomato into your mouth. I have watched you go through your fear of poisoning from this tomato.

Now, I am not asking you to trust me. Just check out what I say. Is this poison I offer you or nectar of truth?

---

*   shakti - Powerful manifestation of energy.

I am not asking you to follow me. I am not asking you to obey me. I am not asking you to think I am the greatest. Just check out what I say. How can you know if you don't check it out?

I am asking you to trust that which reveals itself within you when you let go of every idea of yourself. Let every idea go. If you let all ideas go, in an instant you will see that your idea of Gangaji is not here either. Let ideas of Gangaji go. Let ideas of yourself go. Be willing to be nothing for an instant, and see what cannot be let go.

Have some distrust of your perpetual distrusting. Then see for yourself. No one can carry you to this. You are already this. If you wait for me to carry you, or someone else who looks more like you think the carrier should look, you will be waiting forever.

Postponement is a trick of the mind. I remember many years ago seeing Ramana's picture in spiritual bookstores. First of all, I was struck by the beauty in his eyes. Then I would see his physical posture, and I thought, "Well, slumping like that couldn't be right, so I am not going to read what he says." Shockingly, I thought that his posture actually meant something, because at that time I was very interested in the body and pursuit of the perfection of the body. I found something seemingly imperfect in a holy man's posture, and I used that as a way to postpone realizing the truth which so clearly radiated from his eyes.

Beware of these mental tricks. They are the poison of the myth of the perfected form. You have already eaten this poison and it is still gnawing at you. Spit it out. Then you will see perfection regardless of form. You will see through form. You will have no problem with form.

Do you understand how this is so prevalent in your life? People come to Colorado and are upset that it is dry. People go to Maui and are upset that it is humid. This upsetness is the result of poison. In being poisoned, you miss the mana, the power, the darshan* that is being given wherever one is. Don't miss what is radiating everywhere. Don't continue to be sickened by mental poison. Look deeper than that, and you cannot miss the resplendence.

Don't trust me. Don't even trust that there *is* a me. Go all the way with this distrust and *then* distrust will help you. Don't trust what you see. Don't trust what you feel. Don't trust what you believe. Don't trust what you experience. Cast it all aside.

What remains? What is completely untouched by your trust or distrust?

I am very happy to welcome that here.

• • •

I have a general feeling of fear or mistrust arising in me, but it's not about you.

Fear or mistrust arises. Do you trust your story about the fear and the mistrust that arises? If you do, it is misplaced trust.

As you said, I don't really trust anything.

Well, if you don't really trust anything, what is left?

*   darshan - Emanations of grace.

25

The unknown. What I hear inside is that I'm tired of being told to jump into the unknown. I've done that before, and I've gotten slammed.

You are lying. You have never done this before. It cannot be done. Maybe you have thought about the unknown. Maybe you have imagined the unknown.

Yes, those thoughts *are* untrustworthy. Give up everything, including trust and distrust. Give up both polarities, the whole coin, the whole package.

I am speaking of what has never, ever, been known. I am speaking of what is unknowable. Not unknown until you know it, but *unknowable*.

I'm laughing that for all of the times I have trusted things that have turned out to hurt me, here I am with what is most likely the one thing I could have ever trusted, and it's comical what comes up.

What have you trusted that has hurt you? Some person? Some idea about what that person should give you?

It has been on many levels, even theories and teachings.

Especially theories and teachings! Those are words. Those are concepts. Even if words are pristine and accurate, they are usually heard through the filters of conditioned mind. Then you trust as a child hearing a Sunday school story trusts that God is in the sky and will come down from the sky and pick him up. There is a great sense of betrayal when the child realizes that God does not drop from the sky to rescue him.

Throw these stories away. It is time to grow up and stop wasting your life by pinning your hopes on some story. You have been continually let down. That betrayal is called samsara* or neurosis, and in extreme cases, psychosis.

Here is the opportunity to put every concept aside, however elevated, however sublime, however true. In that nakedness, in true nakedness, there is no waiting for some theory, or philosophy, or image to come to the rescue. Be totally naked, and speak from that.

There is that which is totally, permanently present and has always been so. It can't be given to you. No one owns it to give it to you. No one can own it. You are it.

I don't want to foster your hopes that I, Gangaji, will give it to you. What a joke! How can I give you what you already are? If you imagine that I will give it to you, then you will be afraid that I might take it away.

You might be able to stop me dead in my tracks though.

That would be wonderful. Then I will have done my job, but to do my job is not up to me.

Is it up to me?

Yes! It is up to you. I am waiting on you to do my job. You can catch this fire. Catching fire is possible because already within you the fire is burning. Whether it is a small, smoldering ember or whether it is blazing, you can recog-

---

*   samsara - Suffering in ignorance of one's true nature.

nize it is burning. Recognize the fire and fan it so that it burns up everything– all coverings, all disguises, all masks– and you are left beautifully naked.

There is a fear of nakedness, a fear of being exposed. Mostly you are aware of the garments of shame, and worthlessness, and inadequacy. You assume they are your nakedness, but they are like pieces of cloth covering true nakedness. When I say naked, I mean naked of *any* concept of who you are.

Remove the concept that you are your body. Remove it by truly, deeply, earnestly, alertly, and in surrender, asking, "Who am I *really*?" Not who you have been taught you are. Not who you have believed yourself to be. Who are you *really*, in truth?

No one can ask or answer this question for you. You cannot trust anyone to ask this question for you. No one can answer for you, no one can live for you. You have to discover yourself. You have to see yourself. You have to live yourself. It is that simple.

Just for a moment, don't think about who you are. Don't think about what you need, or what you didn't get, or what you should get.

In this instant of not thinking, truth is evident.

The true teaching is everywhere. Just stop hoping for it to look a certain way, expecting it to speak or act a certain way, and you will hear it. It is everywhere. It is coming off every pine needle.

• • •

You just said that it comes off every pine needle, and in this beautiful setting it is very easy to feel that. What about big cities and cancerous-like developments? It seems much more difficult to feel it there.

When I was first with Papaji, we were in a humble room on the banks of the Ganga.* The walls were mildewed, and yet I was struck by the beauty. Everything was shining. The quiet and the presence were all-pervasive. I thought to myself how ironic it is that in the West we have visions of God sitting on a golden throne in heaven. Here I am in a humble little room with strange smells and sounds coming up from the street and I realize, *Here is God. Here is God. This is heaven. I am in heaven, and who would have expected it in such a poor place?*

The next day he took us for a walk in the marketplace. Such sounds! Such smells! Such grabbing and screaming! Not esthetically pleasing at all, and I wondered, why did he bring us here? It was so perfect there in that beautiful little room. I looked at him and wordlessly he said, "Here too." In that instant, all noise was penetrated by the eternal, abiding silence. The beauty was seen. Even the beggar whose body had been eaten away by leprosy was seen in his beauty.

Perhaps you realize the grace of a moment of beauty. To be true to that grace you must explore it. See if it truly ends. Does it end when you step into downtown Denver or Manhattan? If true beauty appears to leave, be willing to retreat for a moment, one millisecond, and you will see that true beauty is everywhere, emanating from everything.

*   Ganga - The holy river Ganges in India.

I understand it seems harder to see beauty in rectangular buildings, and in fearful, aggressive people rushing about. But if you stop in the midst of that, just for an instant, you will see the buildings and the agitation cannot truly cover beauty. They can appear to. They can seem to, but they cannot *truly* hide it.

Honor the instant in your life where you recognize beauty to be the truth of who you are. Honor revelation by taking one millisecond to check when you assume it has been lost.

It is very usual to honor the thoughts, the emotions, and the feelings. Be unusual and honor that which is deeper that any thought, feeling, or emotion. Let your life be an unusual life of fulfillment, regardless of circumstances, regardless of moods, regardless of discomfort.

People overlook everlasting beauty because they desire to be somewhere different. Somewhere they imagine circumstances to be better. Stop where you are and check.

Check deeper than the physical realm, deeper than the mental realm, deeper than the emotional realm. Then you are open to receiving darshan in all forms, pleasant or unpleasant. Then the satguru speaks to you always.

Satguru is the true guru, the real guru. The true guru comes in all forms and uses all forms. Satguru is your own Self. As guru, as disciple, as giver, as receiver.

Meditation and Practice

Could you say more about what you consider to be true meditation ?

The purpose of meditation is to quiet the mind. In the quiet mind, conditioned responses are exposed and obliterated. Meditation allows the mind to release its fixation on objects, and to rest in its source.

The quiet mind reveals that which is always silent, that which both activity and inactivity spring from and return to, that which the experience of ignorance and the experience of enlightenment spring from and return to.

That is your own Self.

Often what gets called meditation is concentration practice. Like therapy or breathwork or other yogas, concentration can be helpful. It has its place. Now discover what is beyond concentration. Discover what is no object of concentration but is silent awareness itself.

I am not against meditation and practice. I am against the separation of a practice of meditation from life. When the separation between practice and life is recognized as illusory, then your whole life is meditation. Life is silent awareness, and all the events of life appear and disappear in that silence. You are that silence.

• • •

Do you feel that formalized meditation practices are at all useful in discovering this?

Meditation practice can be very useful for calming the mind, and thereby experiencing relatively more peace. However, in time the meditation practice usually becomes an obstacle, because there is both the image of "meditation," and "my life," as well as an image of a "meditator" doing "a meditation." These images are mental traps.

Anything can be either useful or a hindrance. What has been useful can become a hindrance. What could have been a hindrance can become useful. It is not up to me to make this determination for anyone. Discover for yourself.

The opportunity in this moment is to see for yourself if what I say is true, rather than just another theory to be agreed with or disagreed with. The opportunity is to allow your mind to be still for an instant, and then to speak from experience of stillness.

In quieting the mind, there is recognition of endlessness. There is, for an instant, the recognition of what has always been.

Endlessness does not come into being or suddenly become endless. It *is*. It always is, whether there is an active mind or an inactive mind. The purpose of deactivating the mind is to realize that.

• • •

Is it helpful to do things like visualization or body work to help move energy that seems stuck or held?

Finally you are invited to step into the middle of the ocean. At that point all that is helpful is to let go of everything. Every preconceived idea of what will get you somewhere is based on the assumption that you are not already there. You are already there. You are already That.

To immediately discover the truth, let go of every technique to get to truth. Whether it is peace of mind you want, or full, total realization of the truth of your being, let go of every concept that you are not truth. Let go of every concept that you have to do something to get truth, to realize truth. Let go of every concept of who you are, period, and see.

Is wanting to get rid of stuck energy the problem?

The problem is not with the stuck energy. A problem is created when you either deny something or wallow in that something.

Just for this instant, realize who you are.

Now, what energy blockage touches that?

An energy blockage is like a bump on the Earth. It is part of the physical terrain. In your willingness to be who you are, if only for one second, you will see that there is either physical release or not. Bumps are smoothed out or not. It doesn't matter.

In the past I pursued different disciplines, traditional and new age. Although the highs, the ecstasy rushes, had certainly been enjoyable, I wanted something that no formula had been able to reveal. I spent a lot of my time going around to teachers and workshops, and remained dissatisfied. Out of that dissatisfaction I prayed to be delivered. I prayed to realize truth. I wanted truth more than I wanted comfort and pleasant experiences. I wanted truth beyond what my mind could deliver.

That prayer revealed itself in meeting my master, and his words to me were, "Give up every concept immediately, instantly."

I listened to him. Somehow, I had enough good sense to listen to him and not get into an internal discussion about *whys* and *buts* and *what ifs*.

I simply heard what he said, and what was revealed is the limitless truth of one Self. Not *me*, but one Self, the totality of being. The *me* is lost in that. It is insignificant, a minor energy blockage, a bump on the Earth.

• • •

How can one know the Self without study?

What exactly do you mean when you say Self?

Initially the small self, and then merging with the larger Self.

What is the small self?

The form I chose to incarnate in.

Do you mean your body?

My body, personality, ego.

A body can be studied. A personality can be studied. What do you mean when you say ego?

Habits, imprinting.

Habits and imprinting can be studied and the study can be useful. If there is identification of all of those habits and imprinting as who you are, then the study is an obstruction.

You spoke of merging with the larger Self. What is the larger Self you merge with?

With what's infinite. I merge with what's everywhere.

If it is everywhere, aren't you already merged with it?

No, I think there is something before that.

What is before infinity?

A set of experiences.

Who do these experiences belong to?

A personal self first.

Who does this personal self belong to?

The world.

Who does the world belong to?

I believe it's all the same.

If it is all the same, it is infinite Self, right?

Maybe. Oh! Yes...Right! I see!

To mentally understand something is to objectify it, to particularize it, to categorize it, and to note its characteristics for storage in memory. Any "thing" can be studied. Anything that you objectify and believe to be separate can be studied as if it were separate. Totality of being cannot be studied.

What is separate from totality that can study totality? Maybe you can understand personality and bodily functions and natural laws. Self is the totality. Totality is nothing in particular, and the belief that to realize no-thing one must study is a big mistake, and an unnecessary waste of time.

If you believe that to recognize truth, you have to study some system about truth, you are postponing realizing truth in this moment.

You are the totality. This that you are is much more vast than any one mind-stream can understand.

The futile attempt to give characteristics to God, to nothing, or to truth, is a subtle mental diminishing of the totality of being with gross results.

I ask you to consider, *Who is studying?*

The objective would be to know it in a way that it would melt down and not be identified with.

What melts into what? First, in this moment, whether you have studied or not, ask yourself this question, "Who am I?"

Pay close attention. See if you can find any "thing" that can be studied, whether you call it big or small. This *I* that studies the Self. Tell me, where is this *I*?

It's everywhere.

If it is everywhere, how can it be studied? What is separate from it to study it?

You can study something that you want to commit to memory. You can study to be a doctor or a lawyer or a mechanic or a singer. You can study to learn how to read and write. There is nothing wrong with studying. It is a great power of the mind.

Once the desire to realize who you truly are arises, then the habit of studying must be put aside for at least a moment. The habit of seeking yourself in categories and particularizations must be put aside.

Any spiritual study that is worth studying points to the fact that who you are cannot be studied. The truest teachings point to who you are as that which cannot be objectified, and thereby cannot be learned.

Self forgetting is an apparent mental veiling that gives rise to the mental activity of searching. The experience of Self forgetfulness is the source of all misery, and there is great stress in attempting to remember who you truly are. How do we remember or know the Self? The truth is you cannot remember the Self. The good news of that truth is that you also cannot truly forget the Self. Stop searching in your memory and recognize what has been here all the time.

In the instant of ending your search, all studies are released, as everything is released each night when you drop into deep sleep. In deep sleep there is sublime bliss. There is neither remembering nor forgetting. The opportunity in the waking state is to neither remember nor forget, and see what is here when you stop looking for it.

Retreat. Retreat from all studies, all teachings, all conditionings, worldly or spiritual. Retreat from your name, your relationships, your past, your future, and your present. See that all relationships, names, forms, past, and future arise in That. All come and go in That. *That* is permanent, eternal, and is present right here, right now.

Retreat is the open gateway. Walk through the open gate, and recognize true Self.

• • •

What is your own experience of developing bodhicitta?*

Bodhicitta is not developed. It is *revealed* deeper and deeper. There is not for an instant any separation. You, me, it, them, bodhi, awake, ignorant, ego, mind, Self, illusion—no separation. That is the absolute truth.

In the Buddhist path one generates bodhicitta. One way to generate bodhicitta is by the act of giving.

The antidote for the experience of suffering generated by grasping is the act of giving. Very useful medicine. However, this medicine also has its toxic side effects. If there is identification in the giving, there is ego-righteousness or spiritual delusion.

---

*   bodhi - "awake"; citta - "heart."

To discover and live bodhicitta, discover who you really are. An endless ocean of bodhicitta is discovered to be one's true nature.

The essence of the Buddha's teachings is that you are not separate from the Buddha. What came after the Buddha were ways of figuring how to get there, but this trying to get there implies that you are not already that itself.

I understand the dilemma. Obviously, the experience is that you are not that. This experience that you are separate from Buddha, from God, from Truth, is an experience of suffering. It seems real and is believed to be real. Then all kinds of tasks and paths and tapas* are performed to get through illusion to the truth of oneself.

It seems that revelation would be more of a receptive experience, and generation would be more active, both waiting to achieve the full state of being.

If you are truly receptive, you need nothing. In needing nothing, revelation reveals itself. Not as something that was or is to come, but as itself, now and evermore. What you are calling "generation," is a slight misunderstanding.

Bodhicitta or Buddha-mind or Truth is endlessly revealed, not generated. Generation has in its meaning "bringing forth." It wasn't here and now it is.

Truth or bodhicitta is eternally here. This is subtly but essentially different from being generated. Generation requires concentration of effort; revelation requires receptiv-

---

*   tapas - Austere purification practices.

ity. In receptivity there is no waiting; the instant there is true receptivity, there is overflowing bodhicitta.

Creative power is obvious, but that which creative power comes from and that in which creative power rests, is the revelation. It can be named Eternity or it can be named Buddha. Whatever it is named is secondary to the truth that it is always fully present.

Do you understand? This is a very important point. Bodhicitta, like compassion or wisdom, is revealed through realizing what is eternally present.

Religions East and West have tried to teach compassion. Often, the result is suppression of the image of who you think yourself to be, which is bad and evil, layered over with other images of who you think you should be, which are good and just and kind. It takes enormous psychic effort to keep the dark side, or evil self, or negative mind repressed.

The possibility is to realize what exists *before* good and evil– and in that, nothing is repressed. In that, both good and evil burn up. You realize yourself to be neither an evil person nor a good person.

When you are not in battle between generosity and selfishness, you are still. You are neither defining yourself as generous nor as selfish. When you are not defining yourself, freedom is recognized. When there is no attention put on acting out or repressing any aspect of yourself, ironically, generosity is revealed to be your natural attribute.

Let me stress, I am in no way sanctioning acting out negativity. By being willing to directly experience what you fear as your evil nature, by not moving to repress it *and* by not moving to act it out, negativity cannot survive.

Generating or focusing or accomplishing involves a volition of will.

Yes, that's right. Will to see what already *is*. What needs no volition? What needs no creating? What needs no intending? What exists prior to all *-inging?*

One has to sit, to meditate, to reflect.

If what you mean by meditate is to immediately die to all form and to all thought, then I agree. This is essential.

Whatever the practice has been— call it meditation or working in a store or being a parent— it has led you to a point of recognizing "Aha! Here I am up against this dilemma again." At this point you have the possibility of being absolutely still, having no thought of Buddha, Christ, bodhicitta, meditation, goodness or badness. An instant of no mind. Discover what needs no practice to be.

There is an essential experience that must occur, and I believe this is what you refer to when you say one must sit. This essential experience comes most unexpectedly in the willingness to die. It comes in the willingness not to know what your relationships are, what your history is, or what your form is, much less all the permutations of that knowledge.

I mean to alertly not know anything, to consciously not know anything.

In alert attention, your mind can become so calm that the idea of "you" or "mind" is simply no more

• • •

41

By the time the Buddha sat by the bodhi tree, he had tried many practices, and he had left them all behind. Regardless of what appeared to tempt him forward or backward into time, he sat still.

He died to any idea of who he was. His realization is not separate from your realization.

Permanence and Impermanence

Discriminating wisdom recognizes the folly of chasing impermanent things in search of permanence. Whether it is in money, food, lovers, or great spiritual states, it is foolish to search for something permanent in something that is inherently impermanent.

Discriminating wisdom is essential. Without this discernment, there is no possibility of the final recognition of what is permanently here.

Recognition of impermanence is like a thunderclap opening the mind. Not a belief, not a hope, not a theory—but a realization that all of your grasping has been in vain. All of your rejecting has been in vain. All mind activity of attempting to hold, to keep, or to deny, has been in vain.

If you link up realization with particular experience, then in your mind, realization is a thing. No thing is permanent.

● ● ●

I've had experiences from time to time of awakening and bliss that lasted as long as two weeks. But how does one surrender or open to that state permanently?

First make a clear distinction between what is permanent and what is impermanent.

Thoughts are impermanent. They appear and they disappear. At the very least you know that they disappear every night when you fall into deep sleep.

All forms appear and disappear. Even the most sublime experiences are subtle form, and as form, they come and go.

Maturity is the recognition that every "thing" comes and goes. This is the truth. At first it may seem to be a terrifying truth. There is no "thing" that will stay. Surrender in the face of this terror, and recognize the impossibility of holding onto anything. You cannot hold onto your own body, and you cannot hold onto the most desired state. When you recognize the impossibility of holding onto anything, surrender is possible. In surrender, permanent presence of being is revealed.

As you say, awakening has been glimpsed. The experience of bliss that continued for some time is the result of that glimpse. The strong tendency is to attempt to cling to this sublime result. Don't you know this very well? As you feel the sweet experience ebbing or leaving, there may be panic, or a scrambling of mental activity in the attempt to keep it. Of course, as you scramble to keep it, the sweetness retreats much faster.

There is an essential recognition that must occur for a mind-stream to recognize its source. If you try to cling to the result of that recognition, you overlook Self-recognition *now*.

If you attempt to cling to a state of ecstasy, however sublime, you overlook what is deeper than ecstatic experience. And since no state can be clung to, disappointment is experienced again and again.

Why not cling to what is always here? This *can* be clung to. This is eternity itself, outside of time, yet including time. Eternity does not come and go. It is no "thing." It is what all things, including all states, arise in. Bliss and not bliss, extraordinary and very ordinary, comfort and discomfort appear here, in eternity.

Eternity is your refuge. Recognize eternity within yourself. Eternal presence is Buddha-mind. Eternal presence is not becoming Buddha-mind or attaining Buddha-mind. It is recognizing itself as eternal Buddha-mind now.

Regardless of the state occurring, there is that which emanates quiet, openness, peace, and clarity. That is no "thing."

First recognize what is impermanent. I say every "thing" is impermanent, but you must discover this for yourself. When you really discover that everything is impermanent, you will immediately stop looking for permanence in "things." Stop looking for permanence not only in gross things, but also in very subtle things such as ideas, states, and experiences.

The perpetuation of the cycle of suffering is accomplished by continuing to try to squeeze permanence out of some thing which is inherently impermanent.

• • •

I'm unclear about the difference between an experience of that which is permanent and the permanence itself.

An experience is impermanent. There was a time when the experience didn't exist. At some time it appeared, and at some time it will disappear. An instant recognition of that which is beyond experience, an enlightenment experience, is an instant of conscious no-experience.

45

There are many moments of no-experience in a lifetime or even in a day. Because our attention is usually fixated on experienced objects, the ground in which all experience of objects occurs is normally overlooked. Awareness overlooks itself.

Find awareness and you find permanence. How do you find awareness? By giving up the search for awareness as a thing, an object.

Ask yourself, "Who is aware?"

• • •

I think I'm understanding the knot that catches me, because what I'm trying to do is make a concept out of what is permanent so that I can "get it."

Right now find the *I* who is trying.

In the moment that you say that, it's obliterated.

Is it obliterated, or is it revealed to actually be only imaginary?

It is gone. It was imaginary.

Then what needs to be held onto? Who can hold onto anything?

In this instant, nothing, nobody.

Excellent! This is the truth.

But I want to find some way to point myself there when I'm not here in satsang.

If at any moment you imagine you are separate from that permanent presence, see if you can find who is separate.

When the knot is recognized to be an impermanent figment of imagination appearing and disappearing in permanent awareness, there is no knot left to be unraveled.

• • •

You say if things or experiences come and go, then they're impermanent. My being in the state of openness also comes and goes.

The state of being open, meaning feeling open and the thought, *I am open,* comes and goes. What does this feeling and this thought come and go in?

What all impermanent feelings and thoughts come and go in is more open than a feeling of being open.

Awareness is not limited to any particular state. True openness is so open that it includes states of not feeling open. Not, I feel open and therefore I am open. Rather, *I is openness,* therefore everything is experienced.

Then by definition if someone has that glimpse, shouldn't they always be there?

You are always there.

But if that were so, we would all be conscious there.

Consciously recognize where you always are. Recognition is not an attainment of a new state, although recognition does give rise to exquisite, sublime states.

There are traditions that will teach you attainments of states; great, powerful, yogic states. What I am pointing to is who one always *is*.

Anything attained was not here before attainment. What is permanent cannot be attained and cannot be lost.

• • •

You know that appearances cannot be trusted. Shadows cannot be trusted. Images cannot be trusted. That which you have assumed to be solid and real cannot be trusted to be solid and real. Anything that comes and goes, changes or vanishes, ultimately cannot be trusted except to come and go and change and vanish.

If you are searching for what is absolute, for what is permanent, then you must stop looking in what is impermanent and relative. Stopping the search reveals Self as no "where" in particular and no "body" in particular.

If you just hear the words, you may assume some "thing" in particular. If you happen to notice what the substance of words is, and that words themselves come and go, then you will know that words by themselves are not trustworthy or reliable.

However, what these words arise in, what they point to, what they exist in, and what they return to is permanence itself. True, everlasting presence— here, now, and always.

• • •

I'm always afraid of losing, so I must be in the other state.

Conditioned experience alleges that you are in states. In truth, states and experiences are in you. They are impermanently in you.

You say, "Always afraid," but this is a lie.

Can you honestly tell me throughout your life experience there has never been one instant when fear was absent?

That's true. There have been many times when I did not feel fear.

Do you see that when you say, "always afraid," you deny the truth? Can you ruthlessly tell the truth and recognize that your denial of even one instant of lack of fear perpetuates the cycle of misidentification and suffering? Do you recognize that fear is impermanent?

Yes.

Good. Now recognize what is exactly the same in the experience of "fear" and the experience of "no fear." Realize what is permanent.

• • •

Experience itself comes from permanence, exists because of the grace of permanence, and returns to permanence, and is therefore never separate from permanence. No thought or experience or sensation or image you have ever had of yourself has ever been separate from the truth of who you are.

The sublime secret is revealed by releasing your attempt to define yourself in impermanent objects. By giving up all definitions, Self can find itself even in definition! Never lost, never obscured. Buddha in compassion, Buddha in anger. Christ in affirmation, Christ in denial. Then concepts like permanent and impermanent are irrelevant. These concepts, too, are just the play of mind.

What a secret! No mind can comprehend this secret.

Nature of Mind

The mind has to keep spinning to hold your view of reality together.

Since personal reality is mind-created, it can be either a negative reality or a positive reality. You can view the world as enemy or you can view the world as friend.

Of course, a positive reality is much more pleasing than a negative reality. It is actually through a positive reality that you get glimmers of that which is beyond mind-created reality, that which has no need to be created by your mind, that in which all creation arises.

The readiness to discover what is before your personal reality, what is not contingent on your personal reality— what already *is* and does not need practice or support or belief to be— is spiritual maturity.

Spiritual maturity allows satsang to appear in your mind. In your mind you hear the call, "Wake up! Wake up!"

Surrender to that call. Mental surrender is reflection, resting the mind, or not thinking. To reflect means to give up all considerations, all computations, all measurements, and just be still. A reflective mind is alert yet at rest. A reflective mind is open. Then, quite naturally, unexpectedly, and mysteriously there arises that which is reflected upon.

I encourage you to reflect on truth, reflect on freedom, reflect on who you *truly* are. Reflect deeply and then more deeply. Insight and revelation arise quite naturally in reflection. Wisdom and clarity are natural by-products of reflection; of not creating and not following mind activity.

All I am ever saying, regardless of whatever words are used, is to be still. Let all concepts rest and dissolve.

Be still, be quiet, and the glory and peace that is revealed is infinite. This is the message of my guru's guru, Ramana Maharishi, and this is the message of my guru, Papaji, and this is the message of this life, Gangaji.

Silence is an opening where the usual evaluation about past events and speculation about future events stop. When you let all mental activity stop, you make your mind available for the unknown, for your own Self, your true Self, your permanent Self, your eternal Self.

If you imagine there is anything that stands between you and your true Self, please, let us expose it and see what is the reality of it. Is it imaginary, or is it real?

It's my mind.

Where is your mind? Find it right now. If mind is the obstacle to knowing yourself, then we must see if mind is real or imagined.

Where did it go?

Yes, where did it go? Where does the mind go in the moment of investigation?

It didn't exist.

If something doesn't exist in one moment, and in another moment seems to exist, how reliable can it be?

It isn't reliable.

It is not even a reliable obstacle, is it?

I just keep believing in it somehow. I keep supporting it.

How?

By keeping it going.

What is this *it* that you keep going?

My mind, listening to it.

Where is this mind? Find it.

In substance I can't.

When you stop assuming mind is some solid substance, what is it?

It's my thoughts.

When you look at this thought, *It's my thoughts,* what is there? What is there when you actually turn awareness directly towards thought?

Nothing.

If thought is insubstantial and is not there, what *is* there?

Feeling, emotion.

Find the feeling, the emotion, and tell me, what is there?

It's imagined.

Now what is there?

Nothing.

And this nothing?
People have heard the word "nothing," and perhaps have all kinds of ideas about what nothing means, such as blankness, or some other concept of emptiness. I want to know, is this nothing some kind of blankness or deadness, or is it conscious, alive intelligence?

Sometimes it's intelligence.

If it is intelligence only sometimes, it is not a reliable intelligence.

Yes, because lots of times it's clouded.

This that is aware of clouds, and aware of some kind of intelligence that comes and goes, what is this?

That is who I am.

Yes!
What you are telling me is that who you are is that which is aware when there are clouds, and that which is aware when there is clarity. Am I understanding you correctly?

Yes, and I judge the clouds.

Is it awareness that judges the clouds, or is it that judgment appears in awareness as another cloud?

Judgment appears. I don't like it, and then I judge.

Not liking, aversion, and distaste appear. Is this the awareness that you have just said is who you are? Or are these states simply phenomena appearing as another form of cloud?

It is another form of cloud. It is not who I am.

You are speaking the truth. Now just for a moment be very still in this insight.

This thing called mind that you have perceived as an obstacle, is this not just another phenomenon?

It is not who I am.

If I have heard you correctly, you have said that who you are is what is always present; the awareness of judgment, the awareness of mind, the awareness of cloud—*awareness* period.

Yes.

Awareness is always present. Everything else comes and goes *in* awareness.

I get angry that phenomena even come and go.

55

Anger arises and again we have layer of cloud. In the Hindu tradition, these layers are called the veils of Maya,* because the mind, this cloud, has the capacity to appear to break into infinite particles.

I'm very good at that.

That's a *siddhi*, a power. The mind is the greatest siddhi. The mind can imagine something to be so, and then quite clearly recognize it is not so. Isn't this a great power? This is the power of Maya, the power of illusion, the power of trance.

Yes, I see the trance more and more. I see the hypnotism.

Now see the seer.

What does she do that she feels all alone?

She? *She* must be some object you are seeing. Is "she" identification with some phenomenon that has arisen in awareness or is "she" awareness?

Some phenomenon.

Does awareness have gender?

No.

---

*   Maya - The illusion of relative reality appearing as separate self and world.

Correct! No gender. Does awareness have eyes?

Not really.

Does awareness have ears?

No.

Does awareness have form?

No.

The living Heart Sutra* is revealed when you see what is truly here. Nothing! Nobody! Is there ever a moment when this that has no eyes, no ears, no form, no gender, is not totally present?

No. It is always present!

What is always present is who you truly are. Correctly identify yourself as eternally present awareness and take refuge in That.

• • •

I know in my mind that this formulation, this body, all these things that I do are not the truth of who I am. Why—

---

*   Heart Sutra - a portion of the *Prajanaparamita Sutra,* the *Heart Sutra* is a teaching of the Buddha, circa 100 B.C. The essence of the Heart Sutra's teaching is: *Form is emptiness; emptiness itself is form. Emptiness is no other than form; form is no other than emptiness.*

Knowing this intellectually is insufficient.

I know that!

Stop knowing anything. Stop the search for intellectual understanding. Stop asking why. Every time *why* arises, it only takes you deeper into intellect. The only answer for *why* is *why not?*

You are being called to that which is beyond mental knowledge. You are being called to direct experience. You are hungry for direct experience, and direct experience is not found in any formulation of intellect.

Be still, and then more still, and even more still.

Be still beyond belief. Then that which cannot be known reveals itself, both fresh and ancient, beyond any polarity of knowing or not knowing.

What is needed in stillness?

What survives stillness?

Stay here. Let stillness dissolve belief in any substantiality of independent existence.

Then there is no way to really know, because if you're knowing, your mind is interpreting what consciousness is.

There is pure being, which is where individual being gets its power. There is pure consciousness, which is where limited, individual consciousness gets its power. Pure knowing is not *known*, nor is it storable, because it is bigger than what can be known from past memory or categories.

It is immaculate. It leaves no tracks. It is what space is in, so it is even more subtle than space.

• • •

What about insights? Aren't they just thoughts?

Insightful, revelatory thought that is original and pure, coming directly from emptiness, is unmediated by conditioned mind. Insight is the holy child of the conscious union of the mind to its source. From that union spring sutra and scripture.

So these revelations are to be paid attention to?

Yes, they are Beauty, and they reflect Truth.
Speak them. Write them. Live them. This is what poetry is. This is what art is. This is what a true human life is.
In all of the glory of the insights, there is always that which is even more glorious– the source itself. Pay attention to that.

• • •

I have some confusion about this idea that all is That. There is thought, and then there is non-thought. There are these thoughts that are just noisy stuff, yet I keep coming back to the thought that even those are That.

Yes, absolutely.

So it's not necessarily a dilemma?

It is not necessarily a dilemma.

The dilemma arises by following thoughts as if they were the limit of reality. They are not. They are waves in the ocean of consciousness. Our general condition is to focus on the waves as reality. Suffering is then experienced as one wave ends, or one wave is bigger, or one wave is something that another wave is not. In that suffering, what these waves or thoughts arise from, what they are composed of, is overlooked.

The teaching that comes from Ramana and Papaji is to allow the thoughts to stop. Be quiet. Be still. In stillness, the vastness of that which exists prior to thought, prior to wave, as well as after all thought, after all waves, recognizes itself in its limitlessness.

We experience bondage only by our attention on these thoughts that are thought and re-thought, and considered to be reality. The thoughts themselves are nothing but electrical impulses, waves, limited reality. Yet these electrical impulses, these waves, this limited reality, are finally one with limitless absolute reality.

Individual consciousness is always one with pure, unlimited consciousness. Shift attention from wave, and ocean is realized. Shift attention back to wave and tell me, has ocean gone anywhere? Isn't ocean always present with or without wave? Isn't awareness always present with or without object (thought)?

Then even the experience of being bound is a thought, but is still That?

Yes! The experience of being bound is not *really being bound*. The thought of bondage leads to the experience of suffering only because it is believed to be reality.

In the willingness to be still, no one can be found either bound or released from bondage. There is only That; the indefinable, limitless consciousness in which all definitions of bondage and liberation arise and end.

• • •

When do you start forgetting about past, present, and future?

Not "when." Now.

Right now drop all tenses and then speak. Otherwise we will get into a discussion about when or even if you should drop the past, and what might happen then, and then we are back to theorizing and speculating. First, drop everything—just for an instant—and see if anything has been lost. Then speak from direct experience.

I understand that people are often worried that if they drop everything they will then lose their ability to function in the world. In general, however, an acuity of both intellect and memory results from this release. When the mind is not forever chasing images and thoughts of the past, there is greater potentiality for pure intelligence to express itself easily.

Regardless of what I tell you, you will never know until you discover for yourself, right? You will never know how delicious dessert tastes until you taste it. You can read it on the menu. You can look at your friends' faces who have tasted it. You can hear their descriptions. But it is all second hand.

The dessert is your own Self. It is waiting to be eaten. When I say drop all concepts, actually what I am saying is not to pick up a concept. You don't even have to go through the effort of dropping anything. Just don't pick up any concept, and then feast on this that you are.

• • •

It feels like without thought the body doesn't exist.

Excellent! That's right. The experience of body is the result of many past thoughts. There is a momentum to these past thoughts that will carry the body until its natural death. You don't have to continue to think to keep the body going. The body has its own momentum.

The body, as you have discovered, is only a thought body. It is a desire body arising from past desires. Let these desires go, and they are finished in their power to create future bodies.

In Eastern philosophy, Self-realization is spoken of as the end of the cycle of rebirth. The cycle of rebirth is experienced each moment. Simply see that what is born, dies, and recognize yourself to be the seeing itself. The body comes, the body goes. An emotion comes, an emotion goes. Strange phenomena come, strange phenomena go. See what all comes and goes *in*. See what needs no momentum and no thought to be.

The ego is simply a thought based on the assumption that you are a particular body, and this is a lie. All assumptions that follow and support this initial mistaken assumption are therefore also lies.

Letting go of the practice of trying to hold the body together, of thinking your reality, is the beginning. What is then revealed is so secret that it cannot be spoken. If it is spoken, it is already a distortion of truth.

• • •

There is a statement, "Mind is like a restless monkey. To overcome it, recite the sutras." I don't understand if there are any sutras that can overcome the nature of mind.

A living sutra can. A living sutra appears in satsang, and satsang is occurring in the depths of your being.

The spring of living sutras is silence. If you surrender to silence, your mind will be tamed. Silence uses the mind to express itself in sutra.

Living truth, whether it comes from the historical Buddha, or from the beggar on the street, is true nourishment. Drink it, digest it, and then the mind is blissfully subservient.

I once heard it said that religion is the tracks where something alive once passed. In the tracks there may be a great emanation of power and truth. If the tracks can serve to inspire you to turn to truth, then they are to be honored. Follow the tracks to their source.

As a child I used to recite a Christian prayer, and I found comfort in that prayer where I imagined there was an angel beside me, and there was Jesus in heaven. Everything was in order and I would be taken care of. At a certain stage that comfort wasn't enough. I needed to enter heaven itself.

That prayer was a way of taming a child's mind. When childhood is finished, prayers from childhood are not enough. Finally the one who is praying must be discovered.

Sutras arise from revelation. Realize yourself, and you will recognize that Buddha is not someone separate from yourself. The Buddha's words, Christ's words, a saint's words, are all your words, your celebration, your devotion to That.

• • •

Is there a difference between liberation and realization?

Within the apparent levels of mind, multiple differences, hierarchies, inner circles, outer circles, and levels of awakening appear. But when one awakens to what has always been awake, where can difference be found in that?

While there is no need to deny the experience of difference. It is the reality of difference that must be investigated.

Where do categories and levels exist? What is necessary for the maintenance of categories?

Where do the terms *liberation* and *realization* exist?

If your attention is pulled to categorization, you overlook what is uncategorizable. If you imagine differences to be real rather than appearances in reality, you suffer unnecessarily. Discovering reality releases you from the bondage of differences.

I want to understand. To let go and let God.

You have read many words, and maybe you have studied metaphysics, or practiced techniques and disciplines according to different religious dictates. Now you have to directly discover for yourself.

Put all interpretations about reality– or speculations about reality, or conclusions about reality– aside for a moment. Let that which exists prior to any interpretation or conclusion reveal itself. Let that which is untouched by any categorization reveal itself.

Just for another moment, as an experiment, resist the temptation to define it, to philosophize, or to know. Just for a moment rest in that, and see if your understanding can reach beyond definitions.

• • •

So, is being still a dissolving?

Yes. A dissolving of all thoughts, all concepts. A dissolving of all ideas of who you are, or who you might be someday, or who you should be, or who you hope you can be.

Could you explain what silence is?

There is no way to explain silence. You experience silence.

It is not something that you go to and get. If you go into nature, or you go into your room, or you close your eyes, you may feel more quiet. In nature, or in a quiet place, you are not distracted by your usual worries. That peace of non-distraction points you to silence.

65

In silence, you recognize that any efforting arises out of silence and is actually searching for that silence.

If you tell the truth and are very attentive to silence, a profound discovery is revealed. You are home.

Many people stop at relative quiet, relative pleasure, relative comfort, relative happiness. Maybe you don't have a television in your house or you don't go to noisy places; but relative quiet is conditional. If by chance life flings you into the middle of downtown New York, where is the quiet? If it is relative, it is gone. It has been displaced by something else relative. The lasting discovery of truth is in absolute, unconditional silence. Then, wherever you are, you know yourself to be the silence itself, absolutely.

• • •

What I get from the silence is a deep sense of aloneness.

Yes, total aloneness. Aloneness is the truth. If you get that, then there is no question of a belief in the apparent "me" and "other." "Me" and "other" may appear. They are only appearances in the field of total aloneness.

True aloneness is all.

The mental definition or image of *alone* indicates something lonely, scary, needy– something in danger. That is not the direct experience of aloneness. The truth realized in direct experience of aloneness reflects deep peace and love.

• • •

Yesterday after satsang I stayed still. I said, "I'm going to fol-low what Gangaji says, and be still." I really tasted that quiet. At the same time, perhaps because of those tastes, I was more aware than ever of my mental activity. There's nothing I'd like more than to be that kind of full stillness you're speaking of.

But I didn't say to get still or to make yourself still. I didn't say to *do* stillness. I said *be* stillness.

I was doing the first three.

People often imagine that silence means an absence of noise, and so then there is an attempt to suppress anything that seems to interrupt quiet. Stillness *is*, and being quiet is recognizing what is *always* still, regardless of events or commentary on events. Even what appears to be noise appears in silence. Return to that. Be that.

What a surprise, this stillness. In the midst of the turmoil, in the midst of all the mind activity, there is stillness. In the gap between thoughts, there is stillness. Before thought, there is stillness. There is stillness after thought. No thought exists separate from stillness.

Be still. Taste stillness. Be yourself.

The challenge is then to recognize that stillness is *always* present. Simply check by turning your mind inward rather than pursuing its outward flow. Relax, rather than efforting to stop the mind's outward flow. Rest your mind.

I am not anti-intellect, but I am suggesting you give the intellect, or thought activity, rest. Let the mind rest in its source. This rest is nourishment. Intellect is hungry for true nourishment.

At rest, individual consciousness expands and recognizes itself as not separate from the universal sea of consciousness. In stillness, there is no separation between "my mind" and consciousness. Separation is experienced only when the thought, *my mind,* is accepted as reality. Be still and see.

• • •

Be available for the unknown, for your own Self, your true Self, the eternal Self.

Open your mind. Be available for what is unconceived, unimagined, unexpected, unnamed. Opening the mind immediately produces wonderful by-products, but don't follow the by-products. Following objects of experience is the great temptation of the mind.

It is very passionate! It is a miracle!

It is *the* passion. It is *the* miracle. It is *the* immensity. That's right! How beautiful that you can speak like this.

• • •

It's very deep.

No one has ever measured the depth of silence. Try.

Turn your mind to measure the depth of silence. Silence is present right here, right now. Measure it. What blissful activity for the mind.

The Heart of Relationship

I'm facing what feels like a lot of temptation as far as emotional involvement in a relationship. This temptation seems to disappear for long periods of time, and then all of a sudden it's everywhere.

What do you mean by emotional involvement?

Well, attraction. When attraction happens in a natural way, when it doesn't feel sought after, and there's some kind of resonance.

Any problem with this kind of resonance?

No, not initially.

The problem is not the attraction, or the resonance, or falling in love, or even involvement in relationship. The problem is what your mind does with all of that. How can you not be attracted? There is no need to resist beauty.

On one level I see the same beauty on every face around me. Then sometimes there is also a tendency to think that this attraction can be used as some sort of vehicle. Maybe as a vehicle for personal pleasure.

It is important to see the activity of the mind. What you are becoming aware of are habitual mental strategies. Vigilance is the willingness to see everything that arises, how-

69

ever unattractive, including how the mind takes that which is beautiful and fresh and twists it into something which is old and rotten. Be willing to feel the pain which results from the twisting. Unsentimentally, experience it.

Don't follow the tendency to take the beauty, chasteness, and pureness that are freely offered, and twist them into something that can be used. If you use them, they will be used up. Be quiet, and let the twisting burn up.

Karma* can never burn if you are unwilling to see these mental habits. It can be quite shocking to see the workings of the mind. It is very easy to point the finger at what is read or seen in the news about what "others" are doing. It is easy to see how destructive other people are who act and react in negative ways. To see the workings of your own mind is vigilance. To see the thoughts of the mind and not react by either repressing them into the subconscious or by following them as reality. Karma cannot survive the willingness to directly experience whatever arises.

Vigilance must be present twenty-four hours a day. Vigilance is not hard and rigid. It is not some kind of carefulness. Vigilance is not separate from awareness. See what arises in your life moment to moment. Then experience what is behind the arisings.

The fear arises when the mind shifts and becomes focused or attached to another physical form.

----

*   karma - The momentum of past desire.

What is it you are really attracted to in physical form, however beautiful it appears ?

If you tell the truth, you see the real beauty is not the form. Form may be beautiful, and different forms are beautiful in different ways, but what is it you really love? What is it you are really attracted to?

The Self?

It is Self which shines out from form, and without which no form has any animation or even existence. Recognize Self as That which you love, and then there is no distraction from your full attention on that. Enjoy the infinite forms Self takes.

Obviously, there will be some forms you are more attracted to than others. Look deeper to what the source of the attraction is, and you will see. Even as a particular form changes, as all form does, and even if it disappears, which eventually all form does, you will not be distraught. You will not feel yourself to be lost because your attention will not have wavered from Self, the true changeless beauty.

Many people have tried getting away from attractions by going into caves, or going into monasteries, or going onto mountain tops, or just going under the covers. Attraction is present in everyday life as the play of all form— as man and woman, man and man, woman and woman, as old and young, as old and old. As moth and light, as bee and flower— all of nature is a dance of this Self-attraction. See the truth, and temptation to follow habits of clutching or denying will burn in that truth.

If you are afraid of something, there is a tendency to turn your attention away from it. Face the feared temptation of attraction to form. See what is at the root of it. If at the root you find desire for acquisition or control, experience the futility and suffering of that desire. Experience lack of control, experience loss, experience not getting what you want. In direct, unflinching experience, you will see clearly that what you truly love and desire is Self. Self is always shining from the core of your being.

I actually see that quite a bit. I also see the latent tendencies of mind that come up around the fear of growing old alone.

Lie down and experience growing old alone, suffering, and being penniless. Don't waste another moment. Lie down and experience this fear.

Growing old is the death of the hope of eternal youthfulness. Face your death. If you can experience death in a young body, how wonderful. Think of all the time wasted in young bodies on the hope of never growing old.

Experience that fear. Then the rest of the life of your body— whether it be one hour, one day, thirty years, or one hundred years— is lived freely.

The latent tendency that haunts you also serves you. It serves as it reveals the fear of something unexperienced. The invitation is to directly experience what has been rejected. In direct experience, false identification is burned.

• • •

When I am on my own, I experience a lot of the peace that is spoken of in satsang quite easily, and then when I am in an intimate relationship with a man, suddenly there is a lot more drama, a lot more story, a lot more difficulty staying with what I experience as truth.

When you are alone, you say that peace is obvious. Then there is being "with a something." This being with something is subject/object relationship.

Relationship with objects is the ground of drama. In drama, object is pre-supposed as separate from you, the subject. Naming the object "man" begins the characterization of object. In your mind, next come the categories; "me" or "not me," "him" or "not him," "intimate" or "not intimate," "enough" or "not enough." This is only the basic sketch. The familiar drama which arises from usual relationship gets quite operatic. Who is winning, the subject or the object? How to get more from the object? How to milk it? How to squeeze it? How to have the object not disappear? How to have the object disappear? And on and on–

Subject/object relationship is eternal frustration, because what you *really* desire is not the object. What is really desired is that which gives life to all objects, limitless Self. The object itself is simply an object of perception. Since perception is limited, it can only perceive limitedness.

Recognize the play as divine tragic comedy. Your frustration at attempting to objectify truth can be seen as the ultimate comedy. You will have some good laughs. In good laughing, where is man and where is woman? In an instant of true laughter, objectless beauty is revealed. This is Self–laughter.

I do not mean that now you must see everything that looks like a man as "not man." First, see yourself and tell me; when this that you truly are is recognized, is it man or woman? Is it human or plant or rock or tree or animal? Is It limited by any definition that arises in it?

The belief in "me" and "other" reflects deep conditioning. In moments when no apparent "other" is around, you have been graced to recognize expansive peace. Now it is important that the appearance of "other" arises. Now you have the opportunity to discover the true depth of grace first recognized in no appearance of other.

If grace is limited to "no appearance of other," it is a conditional grace. Be true to revealed grace, by seeing if "appearance of other" *really* clouds anything. Be vigilant. Experience how conceptual clouds only appear to cover pure and perfect peace. See from the core of being and you peacefully see through all clouds.

It is time to come down from your mountain top, and recognize satsang in the marketplace, on the street, and in the bedroom as well as beyond space and time. Otherwise, this that you have experienced while seemingly alone is limited.

When you discover what is boundless, you discover what is beyond the experience of either other or no other. This is realization. Regardless of experience, realization cannot be moved.

• • •

And though physically someone can leave me, their consciousness can't leave me because their consciousness and my consciousness are the same, right?

If this is committed to memory so that it will help you in moments of experiencing being left, it should be titled, *Relying on Philosophy in Moments of Need*. What you are saying is true, but so what? If it has not truly been realized, it is only something you want to be true, or you hope to be true, or maybe you even try to make true with an affirmation such as, "I am not separate. Maybe they can leave me in form, but their consciousness is the same as mine."

You can get comfort from affirmation, but I am not speaking of comfort. Realize who you are by forgetting all relationships. Awaken to That. When experiencing hurt or loss, meet hurt and loss fully, completely, and discover in the core of hurt, there you are, unhurt. In the core of loss, there you are, found. The meeting must be total. Otherwise it is an exercise. I am not giving you exercises. I am taking your exercises away.

Truth must be realized first hand. Second-hand information may be all right for a bridge, but finally, you are not satisfied with just standing on the bridge and reciting what you have heard about the other side. Finally, you must know for yourself. Obviously, enormous resolve is required. Resolve and surrender. Enormous resolve is required because past conditioning denies or distorts true desire. Even spiritual conditioning delays your crossing with tales of what is on the other side.

Direct experience, direct meeting, is a radical ending to the search; no excuses accepted, nothing excluded.

• • •

With my lover I tend to open up and then pull back.

So, stop.

I've stopped a lot of it.

Stop all of it. Can you find any good reason to continue?

No.

Good, then stop it. What could be more simple?

I stop and then I sort of pick it up again.

Don't pick it up. Go deeper into stopping, deeper into opening. Open beyond the body, beyond the emotions. True intimacy is beyond the sense of "me" and "my lover."

The open mind reveals the eternally open core. The core does not close. The core does not go back and forth. The projecting and veiling power of the mind creates experiences of opening and closing. These experiences do not affect the pure, unchanging awareness that is your true Self.

Open unsentimentally, ruthlessly, and courageously. With openness there is no discussion of why you can't open, or what is blocking opening. Be finished with the discussion. You don't have to look back. If the impulse to close arises, let that impulse be the signal for no discussion, just openness. You may feel the discomfort and pain of past closings. Opening is also opening to all past closings.

Experience the pain directly, and be finished. End the karmic drama of opening and closing. Whether you stay with your lover or leave your lover, stay open. Opening is not about staying or leaving. Appropriate action follows true opening.

If there is a sense of power in closing, offer this closing power to openness. There may arise the thought, "Well, what if I want to close?" Give up the possibility of closing, and then even the impulse to close is the vehicle for deeper opening. The open mind reflects the limitless openness of the core of being.

• • •

Please talk about making the decision to end a relationship with someone you love.

If you haven't ended the relationship, then you aren't clear about ending it.

What is it you really want?

If you want truth more than the relationship, then clarity naturally reveals itself.

When truth is primary, it is obvious whether the relationship is to be continued or ended. If you place the relationship above truth, then there will never be clarity. When the relationship is primary, you are asking that relationship to give you something it has no capacity to give.

Stop everything. That in which the relationship occurs is far larger than the relationship. It is that which you love in relationship and in everything else you love. It is that which is bigger than any object, anywhere. It is that which is the source of all clarity.

There are deeply painful experiences, and there are deeply joyful experiences. Truth is bigger than all experiences. You are truth itself. Be true to yourself, then all is clear. If there is something that is abusive or sick or distorted in a relationship, it cannot remain hidden in the light of truth.

• • •

When I'm with someone in relationship, I seem to perceive things that are going on with them, and I don't know if it's a projection within my own mind or if it's actually something that's coming from them.

Ultimately it doesn't matter, because it is all coming from the same source. Return to source. Your return to silence is a purification for all mind activity.

I'm not sure which is which.

It doesn't matter which is which. Just be quiet and everything is released. Whether something originated in your mind or in their mind, ultimately it is the same mind, the same source. Return to open mind. Recognize that the presence revealed in open mind is continuous. Your recognition changes the vibration of the whole world and invites the whole world to openness. In that invitation, if there is anything left unburned, it is revealed. Be vigilant to what is unburned, and burning continues.

You experience the suffering of the world as "other." Regardless of experience, it is all still one's own Self.

If you are willing to return to silent presence rather than become involved in the story of who is to blame, then suffering is liberated. Clarity of action naturally follows this instant of liberation.

First discover continuous presence within yourself. That which is *always* present must be discovered. This is essential. When continuous presence is discovered here, where you are, your whole life is a vehicle for discovery of that everywhere.

• • •

My understanding is that a true meeting can only occur right in the present. At the moment there seem to be some difficulties between myself and my girlfriend, and she's asking to work through things. Working through things for her seems to mean going right into the past. I see that only in a fresh meeting every moment can things really be released and resolved.

Be careful not to use the concept of truth as a philosophical weapon. If the past is facing you, do not deny that past. The mastery is in not denying it, not repressing it, and not following it. Then past is realized to be nonexistent. If past is experienced as existing, and is then covered with the philosophical concept that it really doesn't exist, or is not really important, then philosophical concept is being used as a strategy to either deny or control. The freshness of direct experience of the essential nonexistence of the past is not revealed through conceptual knowing.

As long as there is a sense of past and the willingness to face it fully, then past is discovered to be nonexistent. Not believed to be nonexistent, not hoped to be nonexistent, not thought to be nonexistent, but discovered to be nonexistent.

Often, what follows either having momentarily experienced the past as nonexistent, or having heard someone say the past is non-existent, is formulation of nonexistence into a concept. What follows conceptualization is a very subtle– or not so subtle– denial of what is arising. As long as anything seems to exist, face it and *discover* that only Truth, which is eternal, truly exists. When you are willing to fully meet everything as it appears, you discover eternity itself– at the core of all past, present, or future.

If working it out means some kind of endless analysis of who said or did what and for what reason, finally, working it out is useless. Endless analysis is useful only to finally prove its uselessness. What a great relief in that.

As long as your body/mind appears, there is some semblance of the past appearing. When hunger arises and you have the desire to eat, this desire comes from remembrance of satiation of hunger through eating. You have recognized since you first identified yourself as form, from protoplasm to human being, that satisfying hunger continues the organism. There is no problem with continuing the organism unless you mistake yourself as limited to that organism. This is an ancient mistake. Perhaps the original sin.

If you identify yourself as your body, you experience desire as actual need for survival of Self. Of course, your body must be fed to survive, but you are not your body. You survive all bodies. You are not limited to the past, you are not limited to the present, you are not limited to the future.

Drop all identification with limitation and see what remains. Then if experiences of limitation reappear, they are realized to be the great play of Leela.* In that instant, you have discovered the secret which releases you as either the victim of Maya,* or as the aggressor in Maya. This is such a hair-thin edge, and that is the exquisiteness of it.

It has been said that upon awakening, the body can be discarded immediately. If this happens, fine. If it doesn't happen, then participate in the exquisite play of Leela. There may be difficult moments, difficult relationships, difficult experiences. In the core of the worst difficulty, the worst horror, the worst suffering, in the absolute core of all, Truth is discovered discovering itself.

• • •

Renounce the indulgence of following the senses as master. Renounce denying arising sensual experience. In certain disciplines there is an effort to deny sensory experience. In other belief systems, there is the practice of glorifying the senses as if they will fulfill the ultimate desire. Both ways are dead ends.

Neither follow, nor deny. This is the secret. You have tried both paths; earnestly denying, and earnestly indulging. Both the tension of denying sensory impulses and the dissipation of following these impulses cause unnecessary

---

*   Leela - The divine play of consciousness.
*   Maya - Illusion that the play is reality.

suffering. The challenge is to be still, not to repress and not to follow. Then any meeting is satsang and satsang is meeting in truth. The past is always welcome to come to satsang.

There is nothing that keeps you from the realization of your inherent, permanent, present freedom, except your imagination that somebody or something is keeping you from that. Whether that somebody is called "me" and "my personality," or "them" and "what they" did to "me," or "what they might do to me," or "what they are doing to me," it is all just story. Endless commentary based on nothing.

In satsang, someone once said, "Enlightenment is retroactive." It is true. You will see that your whole past is both nonexistent and perfect. Once you recognize the inherent, permanent truth at the core of all experiences, you will see that truth has always been present, and life has always been about that. Sometimes it has appeared in distorted, twisted, ugly, ignorant ways, but still your whole life has always been about that.

This is the divine birth that is everywhere in everyone. Not a special divine birth, but that which can never be separate from divinity. Birth, death, relationships, emptiness, fullness, existence, and nonexistence all come from the Divine, exist because of the grace of the Divine, and return finally into the Divine.

• • •

I've requested that my husband of twenty-four years some-how meet me in this journey.

What I want of him is like a resonant field; it's coming from the heart. His brilliant intellect is so often not in the heart.

The problem might be with the word "heart." Often, the word heart refers to an emotional center. When I use the word heart, I am speaking of the core of being, the actual presence of beingness revealed when everything else is peeled away. The life of beingness. Everything arises from that core. True heart is the core of Being.

The journey to the core is not about past knowledge. The Buddha is not about the past. Christ is not about the past. What is beyond past, present, and future? What is more present than present?

Be who you are. This is what my guru's guru said. To *be* who you are, you must first discover who you are. So the essential question is, "Who am I?" You know who you have been *told* you are. You know who you have believed yourself to be, and all of that is changeable. To be who you are means to be real, finally. Reality is unchangeable. To be real means to be unmovable in that which is unchangeable.

Then your husband does not have to meet you in some place that only you have experienced. He may never speak of a resonant field. He may never speak of the heart. Discover your own Self in him, rediscovered in a different formulation.

By being myself?

Yes, by being true to who you are. If you are totally true to who you are, you already recognize he is your own Self. What great, infinite, amazement in that.

Of course you want to invite him, your own Self, to full potential. Your being true to who one *is*, is the most attractive invitation.

The other revelation I had is the feeling of immense love.

Yes, true love. The emotions that emanate from realizing true love are true emotions, not sentimental emotions revolving around an imaginary you and your needs. True love has never been measured. Immense, boundless love is true love.

• • •

In five weeks time I'm going to get married. I've never considered myself the marrying type; I've enjoyed the freedom of going wherever I fancied. It's bringing up a lot of discomfort.

The play of marriage to someone in particular is a divine play, a symbol and a celebration of the truth of what already is.

Many people have the idea that true freedom is freedom of the body, of doing only what is desired. You have experienced that relative freedom, and you have recognized that following personal desire is limited, that true freedom is something more. There is a more profound freedom than following desires. To think that you are free because you get to do what you want is a childish idea of freedom. True freedom has nothing to do with any desire.

The commitment to marriage is a kind of death, isn't it? The death of one's ideas of "me" and "my freedom."

I celebrate true marriage. When you recognize that who you are is unlimited in the first place, then the limits of marriage are paradoxical expressions of that freedom and beauty. True marriage is a reflection of the inseparable connection with all of life. Be faithful to that embrace regardless of discomfort, regardless of the pull of desire.

Many marriages are merely institutions of servitude and property arrangement. True marriage is a celebration of freedom. It is sangha,* a support of truth. It is the marriage of one Self with one Self.

• • •

Is it a problem if my wife doesn't share that same yearning for truth?

Your partner will catch it from you, or the marriage will be finished. It is that simple.

When I met my husband, and before we were married, all I wanted was a husband. I thought that getting married would be total fulfillment.

I caught the yearning for truth from him. His whole life revolved around truth. How lucky that destiny brought me to a man who loved truth more that he loved me. He served truth more than he served me. He was married to truth before he was married to me. For our marriage to be,

*   sangha - Community of persons in devotion to realization of Truth.

85

I also had to meet truth. Once Truth is met, one cannot help but fall in love.

Let your marriage be in service to that; and then, regardless of the problems, the discomforts, and the trials, it will be a true marriage. If marriage is in service to each other's ego, it is the usual, false marriage.

Serve truth, which is never separate from love.

Longing for the Beloved

Longing for the true Beloved is not content with even the last moment's realization. The Beloved's embrace must be always fresh, always alive, always new.

Whenever longing arises, it may trigger habitual responses of attempting to satisfy the longing with some object, some experience, or something other than itself. These responses are latent tendencies of mind. These tendencies reflect the way we have been taught to deal with longing.

Divine longing is for deeper realization of the fullness of Self. It is very useful. Don't put it aside. Don't move into mental agitation around it. It exposes even the slightest misidentification of yourself as separate from the Beloved.

This longing is a great gift. It is God's gift. It is the longing of the soul, and it will continue until without a shadow of a doubt you are submerged in the Beloved.

Do you mean don't confuse longing with a sense of doubt?

Doubt comes from mental activity. Longing is deeper than mental activity. Rather than diving directly into longing and experiencing it, there is often an impulse to move into mental relationship with it: "What does this mean? Does it mean I'm bad? Does it mean I haven't got it? Does it mean that I'll never get it?"

The longing is a call. A reminder that attention has been turned toward some object.

Longing is your great ally. It is your guardian angel crying, "Return. Return." Don't shunt it aside. Don't try to fill it with ideas, or expectations, or conversation, or doubt. Fall directly into it. It is a waiting vehicle.

Do you mean to open fully to it?

Yes, open fully.

There is often misunderstanding around the arising of longing. To correct the misunderstanding, stop trying to feed it in the hope that it will go away. Thank goodness attempts to get rid of true longing don't work. True longing is a persistent lover. It won't go away with some trifle. It won't go away with some ordinary experience. True longing goes away only in the consummation of itself.

Opening is possible only if you stop all thoughts about it. Put all thoughts aside and allow yourself to *be* longing. Make no separation between you and the longing. When met directly, the longing reveals that which is longed for.

Is the I who longs and the longing the same thing? Are they just a sensate experience?

I longs for itself. Longing is recognized *through* the sensate experience, but its source is deeper than senses. Fall in through the senses. Pass the senses on your way to the source.

If you understand the language of longing, you know a secret language. It cannot be translated. Sufis have attempted to translate it. Hindus have attempted to translate it.

Christian mystics have attempted translate it. Now you must translate it, yes?

It's in the yes! (laughing)

Yes. And it is in the laughter.

Don't hold back anything. Even if you don't hear anything else I say, hear this. Longing is your own soul's call. You are in satsang, so I assume you are here because longing has called you.

Listen.

Give the longing the totality of your being.

• • •

When we find out who we are, will the yearning and longing cease?

Find out and then tell me. Put other's opinions aside. No one else's opinion will satisfy you. I could share with you my experience, but so what? It is more valuable if I can point you to the direct experience for yourself. Then you will speak from your own experience. Not from some belief or some hope, but from your own direct experience.

Are you ready to discover for yourself the truth of yearning and longing?

Yes.

Then turn directly into it.

Be absolutely aware of it.

Stop the distraction of wondering what might be or what might have been. Give everything to pure longing. In this moment, give every sensation, every thought, every emotion to longing. Throw everything you have onto this fire.

There is a beautiful story of a Zen master, who on returning home from market, saw all his neighbors running toward his house with buckets of water.

"What's happening?" he said.

"Your house is on fire," they replied.

They were running to throw buckets of water on his house and to pull his belongings out of the house to safety. He immediately started throwing his belongings back into the burning house. He began to light torches to add to the fire.

Throwing everything onto the fire is required in the call of the Beloved.

If some concept of what will satisfy your longing starts to slip out, or some friendly neighbor starts to pull something out, take it back and throw it all in the fire. Let the fire get huge, and if your neighbors are wise they will bring torches over to their houses.

When a fire is worked up to a certain frenzy, it spreads. Let the fire of longing rage. Throw all concepts of yourself into it. Let everything be burned. Then you will know directly what this longing is. In that knowledge, you will know what cannot be burned. You will know your true Self.

This is a holy fire. It is an ecstatic fire. It is only painful if you put your foot in and pull it out, put your foot back in and pull it out. Jump into the fire!

Don't waste a moment. Don't consider this any longer. Jump!

• • •

Is the yearning greed?

Greed for more objects is a distortion of true yearning. Greed for more sensate experience has to do with the body, with feeding the senses to avoid the call of this deeper yearning. The deepest yearning is desire for that which is Truth.

Recognize that misplaced greed has led only to suffering, and still the yearning has not been satisfied by any object, by any sensual pleasure, or by any attainment. This recognition is maturity.

The usual habit of relating to yearning is to turn to mind activity. You may hide in fantasies of being back with your first lover or entertain fantasies of more new lovers. You may imagine that being back in your mother's womb or returning to the garden of Eden would put an end to your yearning. All of this fantasizing and entertaining hopes for cessation of longing are attempts to escape the call.

The fulfillment of the call of longing is not found back in your mother's womb. It is not found back anywhere; don't look back. It is not found forward either; don't look ahead. Give yourself to the yearning itself, now. This giving reveals the Beloved.

Your yearning is for the true romance. True romance can never be satisfied by mere infatuation or bio-chemical response. True romance is the love of the soul for God. It is the call of the soul for God. It is God's call to the soul. Satsang points the soul back to the source that it yearns for.

Before yearning first arises, there is a numbness of spirit. Somehow, within the course of evolution, desire arises for that which is unknown. The habitual impulse is to fill the space of the unknown with what has been known. This impulse fixates on desire for the lover, desire for the mother, desire for the father, desire for some object promising fulfillment. Forget the yearning *for* something; *be* yearning. Discover that you are what you have yearned for.

By "you" I don't mean any image of you, any sensation of you, any memory of you, or any conception of you. I mean you as you really are. Not as you imagine or feel or sense or believe yourself to be. You as you really are is the unknown you yearn for.

• • •

Are you ready? Have you tried greed? Have you tried lust?

You have tried everything, but have you tried no-thing?

Be no thing. Do you think you know what being no thing means?

Any assumption about the meaning of no thing is based on the false assumption that you are a something.

Believing yourself to be a something, you have worked hard to better that something and maintain that something in the false hope of finding fulfillment in something.

Your longing is a powerful, stark reminder of your failure.

Face your failure, face the longing you have worked so hard either to ignore or to feed with proof of some-thingness.

When you truly face longing and surrender to its call, nothingness reveals itself.

Nothingness is not a dead abyss of space.

True no-thingness is the endless radiant face of your own Self.

• • •

It feels like this longing is a deep wound inside me. That no matter how good my life is, it doesn't change. I've looked at it psychologically and I've wondered if maybe I just can't be happy.

Circumstances can be perfect relative to past desires, but you will not be truly happy until you discover the truth of who you are.

It is good that this perceived wound, this longing, will not let you rest. It will not let you settle for some idea of happiness.

Do you know the story of the princess and the pea? No matter how many mattresses were placed under this very sensitive princess, she could still feel the grit of a pea.

Finally, all the mattresses must be shoved aside to dis-cover what is calling attention to itself. Follow the call to the core.

Plunge into the call, and discover what is the grit that will not let you rest until it is uncovered.

It makes me feel restless.

Yes, it is a restlessness. Without the restlessness, you might have been content to live the lifestyle that was pre-programmed for you. You might have been content with your success, or your compromise, but in fact you are not content. This is divine discontent. Restlessness or discontent holds within itself, within its core, the truth of fulfillment.

You have seen that circumstances have nothing to do with real, lasting happiness. Luckily, accumulation of more, good things has not covered the restlessness, the pea. Now dive directly into the restlessness, and see what is really there.

The story of Buddha is a story of restlessness unresolved by circumstance, wealth, honor, or fame. Buddha was a prince. He had everything, and yet there was something that pulled him from his palace to face suffering and discontentment. He was pulled to discover what is at the core of suffering. He was not pulled to find more convenient isolation or protection from suffering, but pulled to face suffering directly.

Usual mental activity is an attempt to insulate oneself from suffering. With insulation, there is still subtle discontentment. Discontentment is the tip of the longing. Find where the longing originates. Follow it inwardly, rather than following the usual useless attempt to satisfy it outwardly.

• • •

Does longing exist without the mind?

No, but it arises out of that aspect of the mind that is calling and pulling mind back to its source.

Is that when loneliness comes in?

If loneliness is met fully and completely, then loneliness reveals fulfillment.

This is a great secret. Divine yearning will only be satisfied when it is met fully and completely. A great mouth of loneliness may be perceived. If you fall into that mouth, all the way into the core, you are eaten by that which you long for.

I am not suggesting dramatizing or wallowing in loneliness. To fall into the core of loneliness, you must leave all postures of loneliness behind.

The whole world is searching for release from the experience of separation. The worldly search is in reaching for more to acquire and accumulate. Finally, through grace, your search has pointed you back into the loneliness itself. Back into the direct experience of loneliness. Back into what the whole world is attempting to escape. Back into that which you assume to be the beast.

The truth is that you *are* absolutely alone, and in this recognition, deepest satisfaction and fulfillment are revealed. In directly meeting that which is most feared, most dreaded, there is the realization of Home.

• • •

Shyness has been a life-long struggle for me. An overwhelming shyness coupled with a longing to be recognized.

I love shyness. There is real beauty in shyness. We don't have enough shyness in the world. We have all been overly trained in assertiveness and aggressiveness.

In many cultures your shyness would be called modesty, but in our culture shyness is viewed as something to be overcome.

Most appropriately, there is trembling shyness in the face of that Divinity which cannot be captured by the mind, which cannot be grasped by the intellect.

Everywhere I look, I see the cry for Self-recognition, and, however assertive the personality may be, I have never yet seen a lack of trembling in the face of that recognition.

Put your personality aside. Whether it is deemed a "good" personality or a "bad" personality, whether the personality is pleasant or unpleasant . . . put it aside and see what naturally and inherently shines.

• • •

I remember forcing myself to be a cheerleader in high school, performing horrendous feats before crowds of people in order to gain recognition. Still, the emptiness remained.

Without Self-recognition, performing for crowds is never enough. We are trained in our society to believe that if we please enough people, we will be pleased. In pleasing others, still the hungering for Self-recognition remains. Almost everyone has the hunger to be really seen, to be really known. No matter how much the world recognizes you, still you are dissatisfied until you recognize your Self.

How many roads have we all traveled to get recognition?

Celebrities often speak of longing by declaring that fame is never enough. Ten thousand people come to the performance, and still it is not enough. Finally, there is the recognition that true yearning is never satisfied by external references. Then you are prepared to really ask yourself, to finally ask yourself "What is this longing? Who is longing?"

• • •

What I notice is that I'll feel in love, and then it feels too overwhelming.

Yes, fear of love is the same as fear of death. In surrendering to love, there *is* a death. It is the death of objectification. Let yourself get caught by true love, and there is no going back.

Is that the reason that even love is painful?

True love pain is divine pain. It is the pain of completion. This exquisite pain is the explosion of the consummation of God and soul.

• • •

I become consumed with sadness. As I dive deeper and deeper into this sadness, I realize that this too is a story. My tears turn into tears of joy coupled with uncontrollable laughter.

Yes. Oh, yes.

Depth of Simplicity

Reality is not what you think *is*, not what you imagine *is*, not what you have been told *is*. It is not what you believe *is*, not what you hope *is*, not what you fear *is*; but what simply *is*. What *is*, is beyond what can be thought.

To realize what *is*, there must be ruthless investigation of what is transitory and of what is immovable. When I speak of ruthlessness, I do not mean with struggle or effort. True ruthlessness is effortless. It must be effortless. Discipline that is relaxed and ruthless is possible every instant.

I have wished for that kind of discipline.

Even wishing is too much effort. Wishing is a thought, a complication, a postponement.

• • •

I'd like to ask about people who find enlightenment difficult.

The great debate, is awakening difficult or is it easy, is similar to the debate, is awakening gradual or is it sudden. In any era there is a great debate, and the people who are debating are kept very busy. By being kept very busy, rather than just being right here, right now, awakening is postponed.

Forget difficult and forget easy. Who you are is touched by neither. If it is neither difficult nor easy to discover who you are, if awakening is closer than either difficulty or ease, what then?

Who you are is out of measurement. I often point to the ease of awakening only because I am speaking to people who are clinging to the idea of its difficulty. If I meet someone clinging to an idea of ease—

You would say difficult.

Perhaps, because the solution is revealed when the hold of any idea is broken. When the internal discussion stops, the mind is quiet. In silence, where is difficult? Where is ease?

You have spoken about difficulty as unwillingness to experience some things?

Yes, I have said that what makes anything difficult is if you are unwilling to fully experience it. What makes anything easy is if you are willing to experience everything.

What I am pointing to is immeasurably simple. It is more immediate than memory, and closer to you than your own breath. Stop the breath, and it is still present. Breathe the breath, and it is present. Forget everything, and it is present. Remember anything, and it is present. Good experiences. . . *present.* Bad experiences. . . *present.* Denying. . . *present.* Affirming. . . *present.* Sublime discussion. . . *present.* Mundane discussion. . . *present.* All feelings, thoughts, emotions. . . *present.* No feelings, no sensations, no thought, no emotions. . . *present.*

Do you see how simple? You are not separate from your Self. Tell me any experience you have perceived where awareness has not been present? Just this simple recognition can finish habitual searching for your Self someplace else.

When searching is finished, the revelation of what has always been present is self-evident. Not becomes present or grows to presence. *IS* simply, always present.

• • •

It is too simple for my mind to grasp.

Stop looking in your mind for fulfillment. When your mind starts its habitual agitation, treat agitation as a dharma* bell and relax. You will not find your Self in your mind. You find your mind in your Self.

Awakening is experienced as complicated only because you believe depth is revealed in complication. When you are ready to be simple, you will put your ideas aside. You will stop stewing in complication.

If you have led a complicated life, begin right in the center of that complication, the very core, where there is nothing going on. If you like what is discovered in the core, if you are attracted to what is revealed, then bring all your complications to the core. Enormous complications may arise, but when complications meet simplicity, there is no match. Complications dissolve. Complication cannot fight

---

*   dharma - Truth. A dharma bell is a bell traditionally rung to bring meditators back to silence.

true simplicity. Simplicity is too deep. It swallows up everything. Complications only arise as by-products of mind activity. Simplicity is the emanation of truth.

I know that many people are afraid of simplicity. They have an idea or an image that simplicity will lead to stupidity.

Simplicity is not stupidity. It is the deepest wisdom.

I understand the fear of simplicity, but the fear only continues if it is fed with more complication. All that is required is the willingness to be still, to be who you are at the core. Not who you imagine yourself to be. Not who you have been told you are. Any name is too complicated. Even the word "simple" is too complicated. You have some idea of what simple means, and that idea is too complicated.

Recognize the complication of picking up a name, picking up a past, picking up a future. Now put all names aside. Put me aside. Put you aside. Put time aside. Put complication aside. Put simple aside.

• • •

Could you say something about how to live in simplicity?

What is it you really want? Not what you have been told that you want, and not what you think you should want, but what do you *really* want?

I want to be able to relax.

Wonderful. So relax.

(Laughter)

Yes, like that! Easily, immediately. Laughter is the best method of relaxation. No one has to teach you how to laugh.

(More laughter)

That's perfect! It is the perfect, immediate yoga of relaxation. In this relaxation, what do you realize?

I feel an openness. Do I just come back to this every time I lose it?

The image or thought of leaving is the tensing of the mind. Obviously, the tensing of the mind is a strong habit that has been supported by family and teachers and culture for quite a long time.

When this habit arises, relax. In openness, there is no limit. Everything that is searched for in efforting with the mind is revealed in opening the mind.

This is a great secret, a great irony. All of the searching, all of the struggling, all of the efforting to find your true Self, is naturally revealed in open simplicity. Keep laughing. There is no time to complicate matters when you are laughing.

Physical relaxation is very agreeable, and obviously, if you physically relax, there is also some mental relaxation. For deeper mental relaxation, recognize that following a thought takes some effort, some attention.

Do not drift into a trance or fall asleep. Recognize where deep sleep and absolute wakefulness meet.

Usually in wakefulness we are conditioned to follow thought, "It is time to get up, time to remember 'me' and 'my story'; what I am supposed to do, what I didn't do, and what I should do better."

This dialog is usually called the waking state. In the deep sleep state all of that conversation is finished. There is no "me." There are no relationships. Bringing these two states together rests the mind while remaining alert. Reveal your Self to your Self as needing no thought to be, no name to be, no form to be.

I am pointing to Intelligence itself in full potential, awake to itself. When attention is free and open, mind cannot veil Source.

•　•　•

Yesterday during the meditation a little click happened, and the "my's" and "me's" and "mine's" all disappeared.

A *little* click? This click is the end of the world!

There is just a resting happening; no fire, no explosions.

In the center of fire, there is a clear, empty core. That is peace. That is the *I* of the fire.

Somehow it seems really simple.

Yes. What is more simple than the clear core of fire? It is so simple, and yet there is no end to the colors that arise from it. There is no flame, no burning, no manifestation of fire, no form of life, without the core of simply That.

Awakening in the Dream

You are already free, pure, uninterrupted consciousness.

Somehow in the play of yourself, of consciousness itself, there is a veiling of the inherent truth of freedom. Consciousness somehow hides from itself and pretends it is lost. In a certain moment in the play, there arises the desire to end the game of hiding and begin being eternally found. The desire to be found is the desire to awaken in the dream.

I am not here to teach altered states or yogic powers, or even to teach techniques to overcome fear and despair. I am simply here as your own Self to point to that which is found in the core of all being.

• • •

It is such a self-destructive, violent, greedy world that we live in. My question is: How do you live in this kind of world and not feel separate from it? How do you keep an inner balance, an inner peace?

The only way possible is to awaken to what is untouched by "the world."

I'm trying, but it's hard.

If you are overly concerned with the world and its craziness *out there*, you are over-looking the craziness, the violence, the suffering, the separation, and the absurdity within your own mind. It is easy to target world and its faults and its madness. In judging world to be separate from your own mind, there is massive denial.

Where is the horror within you? Willingness to stop looking outward is the willingness to awaken in the midst of a nightmare. Don't dissociate from the nightmare; awaken in it. Have you ever had the experience, while in the sleeping state, of awakening in a dream, in a nightmare?

Yes.

Excellent. You know the answer. Awaken in the nightmare in which you tell yourself about a world that is doing something to you, a world disturbing your peace.

Once you awaken, what's the next step after that?

Awaken and tell me. What good does it do for me to tell you the next step?

Your pre-occupation is with the nightmare and how to escape from it. I am asking you to put all attempts to escape from the nightmare aside, and awaken in it now. What you awaken to is that which has never been asleep.

You are exhausted from your attempt to flee the world. Your exhaustion is the signal that it is time to awaken. Awaken in this nightmare of demons who seem to be chasing you. Let the demons be liberated.

If you have the courage to turn and face the demons that have seemed about to get you, what a revelation! When you finally face your demons, you discover who they are, who you are.

• • •

There is much communication these days about the dimensional shifting of the Earth, planetary ascension, and things like that. Are there some things you'd like to say about that?

In this time of enormous change, there is a great opportunity available. I have traveled over the world speaking to people in many countries, and every place I've been I see a kindling of the desire to realize truth.

I don't pretend to know the outcome of humanity, but I can tell you there is a great quickening, and you are not separate from that quickening.

There is a particular mind-set that is an enormous obstacle to realizing truth. That mind-set states that realization is either something that happened to someone else in the past, or something that may happen for you some time in the future. If you give up both past and future as separate from right now, you can see what is possible in this moment.

I am not pointing you toward conceptual understanding. What is available is deeper than intellectual knowledge, and it is yours by birthright. It is yours because you are called to it, and that call has invited satsang into your consciousness.

Don't miss this opportunity. What great luck! In your lifetime, in this year, in this moment, you have the absolute potential and absolute capacity to realize who you are.

Don't waste time. Get to the core questions. Expose any latent beliefs in separation between you and God, between you and truth.

You have a great role to play. It is time you play your role and stop rehearsing. Stop imagining what the lines are. Stop waiting for something in the future. The future is here now. This is your cue. You're on.

• • •

I'm sitting at your feet today because I need your help. I'm willing to let this fire consume me entirely.

Spiritual fire is your own Self consuming the illusion of *I* as some *thing* separate from anything else. Just be as you are. Simply, fully being is not learned or attained. There is no end to being who you are. There is no end to the depth of it, and no end to the revelation of it. All teachings and attainments come from some revelation of that who one is.

What is so beautiful is that this process of revelation happens whether I call myself asleep or awake.

So don't call yourself either. Don't call yourself anything. As long as you call yourself asleep or awake, you are playing shallowly within the realms of the mind. Extremely shallow is *I am asleep*. Then you may drop into a more profound realm where there is the revelation *I am awake*, but pretty quickly you see the limit of any naming of *I*.

It is important to have the experience *I am awake*, but as it comes, let it go. This experience is just the spring board. *I am awake* is just the other side of *I am asleep, I am ignorant*.

Who is awake? Who is asleep?

This question plunges you into the depth of being where awake and asleep are left far behind. Don't play only in the shallows. The depth of being is calling you.

Sri Ramana said, "It is not the Self that becomes realized. The Self has always been realized." Realize the Self is realized, and then Self-exploration begins.

For someone who has relied on the workings of the intellect, to see deeper than intellect can be a great challenge. Many fears can arise; the fear of being stupid, the fear of going blank, the fear of being nothing, the fear of not existing.

Yes, don't exist. I recommend, if only for an instant, give up the struggle to exist.

· · ·

I find it really difficult since it seems that there is a game plan here to survive, and if I'm going to survive, I have to play the game. To find the time and the quiet to really be able to do the internal work on myself is difficult.

Retreat from everything for five seconds. Close your eyes for five seconds. Drop everything, and just relax. Just be. Simply be.

Do not try to get something or to get rid of something. Do not try to accomplish anything.

Just be immense simplicity.

If you are attracted to this simplicity, if simplicity reveals something that you have been searching for in either acquiring or in accomplishing, then take the next step.

Discover where– in any moment– does this that is revealed in these five seconds go? What are its limits? What are its boundaries?

There are none.

Excellent!

That's not safe somehow.

Not safe? Do you imagine there is safety in doing what your culture says you should do, or in rebelling against cultural injunctions? There is safety only in boundless truth of being, because here there is no need of safety. This is foreground, background, above ground, below ground. This is the ground that is groundlessness.

We know that in the past, certain realized beings would shout the truth and then be shot down or burned at the stake. Yes, this can always happen. So what? You have tried to keep away from truth, or to deny truth, and what are you left with? You may even have memories of being shot down or burned for daring to speak the truth, but look, you are still here. You are still here! Truth remains! Bodies can be shot or burned; Truth prevails.

Only your body needs safety, and of course, there is finally no safety for any body. Eventually every body will be finished. Before your body is finished, recognize the truth of who you are. Then there is no need of safety.

Who you are has no need of anything. You are the fulfillment of all needs. Not your image of who you are, or your sense of who you are, or your feeling of who you are, or any idea of who you are. Those are all objects in the mind. You are the awareness that those mental objects appear in.

How did you find that?

I found that by looking into my guru's eyes. I was attracted to truth, and I recognized I had done as much as I could do with my own ideas of how to find truth. I looked into his eyes, and in that meeting, the whole cosmos was revealed.

He stopped me in my tracks, and stopping me is his gift to you. He named me for the river Ganga, because I met him on the banks of the holy Ganga. When he named me he said, "The Ganga must flow in the West." Now his body is too old to travel as much as he would like, so he uses the Ganga to flood the West.

I'm very moved. I feel like I want to do this every night.

Yes. Very good. Not just every night though–every moment. Never leave satsang. Satsang is the truth of your being. It is always with you.

You are saying, "I don't ever want to be separate from who I am." You are not ever separate from who you are.

• • •

The first satsang we had here you asked me why I was here. I thought, "This is real. This is not some new adventure. It is real."

In that first satsang, you heard from the depth of your being. Hearing occurs when all inner dialog stops. By stopping all commentary and simply being here, you hear what could never have been heard before, no matter how many times certain words have been spoken.

Do you hear? If you do, you hear the heart speaking to itself purely and simply; penetrating all supposed barriers with its willingness.

If there is something at stake, some fear, or some belief that something has to be maintained, you will be too busy attending to that fear or belief to hear. Too busy to recognize what is beyond fear or beliefs. Too busy to realize what needs no maintenance to be.

You must have just said something important, because my heart's beating so strongly right now.

It is in what you heard.

Yes, but I don't know what.

It cannot be captured.

I feel a bit holding back.

Recognize where there is no holding back. Let the body get even more tense, and then in the midst of tension, recognize what is untouched by tension.

This opening is not physical, although there may be an enormous physical release as a by-product. Recognize what is always open.

It's laughing and crying and . . . everything.

Yes. It is finally discovered in everything. It is in laughing, crying, joy, grief, ecstasy, sadness, emptiness, fullness, you, me, this, and that. It is even in past, present and future.

There is enormous physical, emotional, and mental release when that which has never been contracted is recognized. If there is an attempt to cling to physical release, or emotional release, or mental release, what is always open is again overlooked.

In the usual mode of conditioned identification, thoughts, feelings, and experience are referenced for Self-definition. These are traps.

You are the indefinable source of all feeling, all thought, all experience.

Yes, the heart beats very rapidly in this revelation.

• • •

What you are talking about right now, I've heard and I've read about many times. But as you were talking, I felt as if my whole body was burning.

Good! Until you burst into flames, you have not really heard. You imagine you are hearing it if you hear the words. You may intellectually hear, but when you are really hearing, your mind catches fire. True hearing penetrates to the core.

• • •

Gangaji, I really want to awaken, and I go in and out of how strong my desire is. Sometimes it's my total prayer, and then I become scared to do what I think I must to do to awaken.

What must you do to awaken?

I don't really know. I know I've got a lot of ideas of what I think I have to do.

You need do nothing to awaken. Nothing! This is the last thing you expected! You never thought to have this idea!

Searchers everywhere are scurrying to do something to get awakeness. Searchers are reading, efforting, and practicing to awaken. If it is as complicated as doing anything, then the implication is that you are separate from that which is awake, that which is eternally awake.

Don't do anything. Don't even do not doing anything. Be absolutely still. Let the activity of the mind retreat to the core of stillness. In being absolutely still, recognize what is absolutely still.

In stillness, there is no movement of the mind. In no movement of the mind, there is no mind. There is only That, who one is.

When there is no movement of the mind, there is no trickery possible.

• • •

I know I can't continue in the same way I have, that it's non-sense. My barrier seems to be the fear that I ultimately have to give up I.

You do!

I know that, and my question is, Do I just sit with that?

Run headlong into that *I* that must be given up. Find it. Quickly, where is it?

It's in my head.

Where in your head? In what part of your head is it hiding? Report from there immediately.
Can you find it? This *I* that has to be given up. Is it there? Quickly!

I don't know. It's a bunch of thoughts. (laughter)

This is the joke! Where is this *I* that must be given up, if all you can find is the thought of *I*?

I don't know. I've formulated it. I've—

In this instant, allow any one of those formulations to sink back into its place of origin.
What is lost?

Nothing is lost.

When a formulation arises, what is gained?

Nothing really.

Excellent.

I know that, and I still do it.

The formulation *I know that* has arisen. A knower has arisen as a formulation. Allow the formulation *I know that* to dissolve back into its unformulated state. With ending the *I know* formulation, where is the *knower*?

It doesn't exist.

Has anything been lost in the dissolution of the thought of *knower*?

There's nothing lost.

There is nothing to lose. What is fear now?

Right now, nothing.

Be still then. Be quiet. Every time a formulation arises, even the concept that you have to get rid of the last formulation, recognize it as mind activity, as noise. Rather than embellishing upon the previous formulation, let all mental activity cease.

Living life through formulation doesn't work, does it? You have tried endless amounts of formulas, but, finally, you reach a certain point where you realize there is nothing to be gained by any formula of who one is. At that point, there is a natural quieting of the grasping tendency of mind. Mind can open, mind can rest.

Open mind is no different from pure consciousness. At the instant of opening, the truth of limitless consciousness is not veiled by mental formulation.

What is revealed?

Joy! Peace.

• • •

I feel the stillness, but I still feel the tension, and I still don't feel awake.

Where do you check to see if you are awake?

Do you know somewhere? Oh, that would be great!

I can tell where you are checking. You are checking sense impressions. You are checking thoughts based on past conclusions. You are checking that which changes to find that which is changeless.

You are the stillness that is eternally awake. Stillness is full, alive, limitless silence; true emptiness; boundless pure intelligence.

You are describing a sense of separation from that. There is you, and there is the stillness. Dive into that stillness and tell me, where are you, and where is the stillness?

I definitely feel separate. I feel like there is the mind, and then there is the heart.

Yes, you *feel.*

117

Let's examine your idea of mind and the reality of your feeling.

When you say "the mind," what do you mean?

It feels like tension.

If it feels like tension, relax. Now where is the mind? Is it there or is it gone? Is there a mind there unless you say there is?

I don't feel like I can consciously let go. It's like I have to do it by accident.

What you can consciously do is notice how you are holding on. Then relax. Unclench your mind. If you are waiting for an accident, well, yes, you will relax when your body dies. The exciting prospect is that you can relax now. You don't have to postpone it. You don't have to wait for the great accident.

The thought, "I feel this or that, and this or that therefore means" is not reality. If you don't follow that thought as if it were reality, where is the power of that thought? By "mind" I mean all sensory experience that ends in interpretation and conclusions. Ask the question, "*Am I?*" and see *Are you?* Can you tell me that you are not?

It seems like there are two things going on right now. The mind is going to town on wanting to understand, and I can feel in my being that there is no way the mind will understand.

Once you know in your being that there is no way the mind will understand, then you are at the gate of surrender. At that gate you can stop following the impulse to understand with the mind. If you let the struggle go, it is really over.

It just feels like an energy that's tensing.

Relax; mentally relax. Tension arises in the attempt to cling to that energy as if the energy were who you are.

I am feeling it relax. The tension that I had when we started is gone.

Yes, but have *you* gone anywhere? Are you aware of the awareness of feeling?

Is awareness of feeling changed by whatever the quality of feeling?

Tension comes and goes. Awareness is permanent. Recognition of permanence heals the suffering of misidentification.

Who you truly are never moves; therefore, it cannot be lost. You cannot lose yourself. You can experience the loss of IT if you conceptualize IT as an *it*. Regardless of experience of feeling, you are here always. Stop looking for an *it*. Stop trying to find *IT* in a particular feeling, and see what has never moved.

See that whoever you imagine yourself to be changes—comes and goes. Who you are is the permanence.

What a burden released! When this burden is released, your intellect, your memory, and your individual intelligence is used by truth in unknown and unexpected ways.

• • •

Is awakening a gradual kind of deepening and returning to that place?

It has been gradual, hasn't it? How many moments of awakening have there been in your lifetime? So many precious moments in all kinds of circumstances.

There is an instant that is like lightning where what is realized, is realized to have always been present. This lightning bolt, this realization of what is and always has been reveals what does not pass.

Ecstasy and laughter and tears are all by-products of that realization. If you try to cling to any by-product, you will once again experience the cycle of loss and then search for release. Yet regardless of experience, what is always present *is always present.*

Is that realization with you around the clock?

Yes. It is myself. How could I not be with myself?

Was it in your eyes a gradual awakening?

In the moment it revealed itself, I realized it has always been.

If realization were of something new, then it would be subject to getting old. Something that is not here in one time must be subject to not being here in some other time.

I realized that in looking for Self, I had been overlooking Self. From that out-of-time realization, certain experiences occurred. Experiences I had never had before, and never could have imagined having, occurred. But realization is deeper than any experience. Realization is of what is and has always been.

There are experiences of sadness, experiences of happiness, experiences of ignorance, and experiences of enlightenment. These experiences are all secondary to the truth of who you are. Throughout these experiences there is underlying, abiding truth.

In your attachment to keeping certain experiences and getting rid of other experiences, you have simply overlooked the abiding presence. In overlooking truth, there is suffering. There is enormous pleasure in life, and there is enormous pain in life. In focusing on either the pleasure or the pain, what is overlooked is that which is untouched by either pleasure or pain.

You can be happy and you can be sad. You can be right and you can be wrong, but without Beingness itself, none of these can exist. First, primary, foremost, and finally, there is Beingness, before human being, before animal being, before plant being, before mineral being, before cosmic being. Beingness has never gone anywhere.

Recognize yourself as that consciousness which pervades everything as Beingness. What a treasure is revealed!

In this recognition, there is no grasping. What could be grasped? You are overflowing. You have always been overflowing as the truth of universal *Beingness*.

You may see what looks like people, what looks like trees, what looks like flowers, what looks like insects, or what looks like demons, but in Self recognition it is seen that what is at the core of all these appearances is your own Self. What a meeting this is! Self to Self.

• • •

I've heard you speak of "demons" that may arise as one begins to awaken. Can you explain what you mean by that?

As one begins to awaken out of the deep trance of misidentification, surrender to what is prior to all thought, feeling, emotion, and behavior is possible. By opening the gate of surrender, suppressed subconscious beliefs, the demons that have been denied for eons, often appear.

The ego is formulated by past thought. Its existence is predicated on a past. As you begin to awaken and relax and surrender into the truth of now, having nothing to do with past, subconscious thought may appear.

My teacher, Sri Poonjaji, speaking in Hindu terms, says that when you begin to awaken, all the gods and demons of your past come to reclaim you. If you recognize these gods and demons to be mind-created, what power can they have? Let them come. Latent tendencies arise to be burned up in the light of truth.

These tendencies, I notice, are so set from early childhood. Is it worthwhile to go into therapy to have a real look at why these wounds are there?

Whys are resolved in insight when you surrender to that which has no tendencies.

Therapeutic modalities can be helpful in bringing the mind to the gate of surrender if the therapist has directly experienced surrender. The appearance of previously denied or suppressed experiences and states is the opportunity to open to greater depth of being. Insight as to *when* or *how* or *why* naturally follows true opening.

When you are willing to directly experience woundedness, with no idea of why, or when, or how, miraculously you discover that no one is wounded.

So, if the experience of the wound arises, do you dive into this wound?

Yes! Dive, not into the story of the wound, but into the experience of it. Let go of the story. The story is what keeps you feeling bound by experiences of being wounded.

I've been so curious about the story because I seem to find insight there. Is that the trap?

Direct experience brings enormous insight. Allow insights to come.

The secret is not to cling to any state. Let all states pass through you. States you have feared and states you have desired will pass through you. Don't attempt to cling to or reject any state, and in that, directly discover what they pass through.

So it's automatic that the insights are going to come?

The insights come with release. Insights under insights will come.

All is in your imagination! Now, isn't *that* a burden released?

*Why do I keep waiting for the right moment, the right cir-
cumstance?*

The right moment is this moment, wherever it reveals
itself. Just in this moment, now, recognize *I* with no appen-
dages, no predicates, no qualification, no measurement, no
particular location.

• • •

*I see my resolve rise and fall and ebb and flow, and I wonder
whether resolve matters at all, as it relates to waking up.*

Here is a story that Papaji tells.

An Indian princess was very interested in awakening,
and every night she would slip away to visit her guru in
his hut to hear divine teachings. Afterwards, she would
have to slip back into the palace because it was not allowed
for women to go out alone at night, much less to meet with
a guru for the purpose of awakening. It could cause a lot of
trouble.

One day someone came to her brother and said, "I must
tell you that your sister is dishonoring the family. She is
having a love affair, and each night she slips out of the palace and goes to meet her lover."

The brother was incensed. So that night he took his bow
and arrow and followed her. He was going to kill her and
her lover.

As he looked into the window of the guru's hut, the
guru was saying to the princess, "Come very close to me.
I'm going to whisper to you the very word that will finally
dispel all illusion."

She went very near to him. The brother pulled the bow back and took careful aim. Just at that moment, the guru spoke the word and the brother awakened.

He had had no resolve to awaken. His resolve was actually negative and destructive. He was lucky beyond luck to be in the right place at the right time, even if for the wrong reasons.

At this moment you are in the right place at the right time. Take aim with your attention, whatever your reasons for being here. Resolve is even much more reliable than being in the right place at the right time. If you truly have total resolve, every place is the right place. Every word points to the secret word all the time.

Ask yourself, "What is it I want? What is it I *really* want?" Recognize what is wanted, finally, when all is said and done. Be very truthful. At the point of asking yourself this question, don't be willing to lie even the smallest bit.

If what you want is some other relationship or some more money or a better something else, then ask yourself, "What will that give me?" When you get an answer to that, ask again, "And what will *that* give me?" If self-questioning reveals that what you finally want is truth, or peace, or freedom, then point all of your desires into that one desire. Cash in all your other accounts. Put everything on the table for truth, including your body, your history, and all your relationships.

This is resolve. Anything less than this and you are somehow hedging. It is important to see if you are hedging. Now see what it is you really want and what you are willing to give for it. I suggest you give everything. It all belongs to that which you finally want anyway.

Give up every concept of ownership; your house, your mate, your children, your body, your mind, your fear, your courage, your life. Put it all on the table and then see. In other words, make yourself irresistible.

It is important to see if there is lack of resolve. It is important to see if there is even a hint of nihilistic cynicism or falling out of love with truth. Recognize anything being held back. Everything that can be given, give. Give it all, and then you are left naked. In nakedness you are unborn.

I find that resolve withers in the fear of the unknown.

It is not the unknown that you fear. Your fear arises from your imagination of what is in the unknown. You have some subtle image of what might lurk in the unknown.

There is no-thing there. It is unknown. Unknown is unconceptualized, unborn. Truth is unknown, unseen, uncharted.

Give up the lie that you can conceptualize this moment. What an unnecessary burden this lie is. One day the body is finished. At that time, where is your accumulation of concepts?

When you recognize the unknown to be here right now, you recognize pure potential. Before that recognition, there is speculation about what you should do, or what you could do, and there is obsessive rumination about what you did do. Put it all on the table at least for one instant. Then the unknown face reveals itself. See if the known can hold a candle to that.

• • •

It's been very confrontive to look honestly and assess where I am.

Yes, where are you? This is the question. When you really look, what do you find?

Well, I feel myself in you, and in this body of people.

Yes, you are not limited to your body. Excellent.
Now tell me, right now, in your experience, can you find a place where you are not?

(hesitation) No.

Why do you hesitate to shout what is true and self-evident? What do you gain from keeping this declaration hidden?

Realize that you are that which is everywhere, and you realize that any boundary that appears to separate you from anything is illusory. A feeling or a thought of separation is illusion. As illusion, thoughts and feelings arise and disappear. You are that which does not arise and does not disappear. You are present regardless of thoughts and feelings.

Even if you sense separation, this sense cannot be perceived without your presence. Eventually this sense will disappear and another will appear to take its place. Then this other sense will also disappear, and on and on. You are what is present when senses appear and what is present when all senses disappear.

I feel like I know it, but I don't feel like I'm able to live it.

You are absolutely able to live it. You *are* it. It may mean some discomfort, but so what? It may mean not always feeling a certain way, but so what? What is it you want, *really* want?

I would say I want a continuous state of grace, and to extend love to all my brothers and sisters.

No state is continuous. If it is something that is not here now, it is already not continuous. If you are looking for that which is continuous, you have to see what has always been omni-present; omni, eternal presence.

I welcome this.

"Welcome" means come in, the door is open. Don't close your door if a particular wind blows through that you don't like.

Once clarity has been revealed, once the essence of being is revealed as no-body in particular, but that which is eternal and omni-present, there is no more excuse for chasing the tail of illusion.

When you discover yourself to be that which cannot be either limited to or separate from any particular, peace radiates to all particulars.

• • •

This is available to you. What animates this phenomenon speaking to you is no different from what animates the phenomenon called you. Mine was not a particularly noble birth, certainly not a particularly noble up-bringing.

Of course, even though I am just like you, you can still imagine that I am different. That I am luckier. That I have better karma. I have had horrible karma, just like you. Yet I also have the wonderful karma to have satsang appear in my consciousness, just like you.

Don't make any more flimsy excuses, or postpone awakening to some time when things are better. It is here. It is now. It is you.

Facing the Fear of Death

The way death and the fear of death are usually seen in our culture is a clear indication of deep misalignment with truth. Because of our conditioning, physical death is seen as *the* problem. In actuality, facing the reality of death of personal identity is an immense opportunity to directly encounter eternal, undying presence.

There is a strong conditioned belief that a psychological entity is located as some body. In truth, there is no real psychological entity except as an image or a thought coupled with physical sensation.

When fear of death is directly investigated, it is discovered that only form is born and dies. Consciousness is free of formation, free of birth, free of death.

• • •

I have the experience of a continuing dread of death that just hangs around me like a cloud.

If you invite the cloud called death closer, you can experience it directly. In this extraordinary experience, *what dies and what remains* is discovered.

How do I do that?

By being still. By neither repressing nor following any thought that arises. By not moving the mind in any direction. By ceasing all attempts to escape.

Where is this thing called death?

It's squirming right now.

Find it. Go into it with your consciousness. What do you discover?

A sensation.

Now meet the sensation directly. What is at the core of this sensation?

It feels like sadness.

Meet the core of the sadness.
Be aware if your meeting the core of sadness is deflected by a mental discussion about the sadness.

It just feels like a deep, old grief.

Without qualifying, evaluating, or measuring, continue into the core. Directly experience that which is at the center.
What are you experiencing?

It's like a long thing. A sensation of a pole that sits in a cemetery.

An image is the result of separation between you and the sensation. With any image there must be someone sensing and something sensed. I am speaking of being right inside the sensation. Leave the boundaries separating you and it behind. Release all imagery and dive into the core of the sensation.

I find myself going into it, then bouncing off and pulling back.

You are describing a mental image of a strategy used to avoid direct experience. When the image of bouncing starts, continue to relax. Drop into the core of the grief that you have dreaded and avoided. Other images or names might arise, but for now—rather than speculating about the grief or analyzing it or overcoming it—discover what is present at the core.

In open meeting, the nature of all phenomena, subtle or gross, is discovered directly. Any phenomenon can be met directly, whether it is the emotion of sadness, or the thought of "me," or death itself.

This is a great discovery. I am simply saying to put everything aside and discover the underlying nature of everything.

The usual strategy is mental movement away from direct experience and toward a technique of overcoming, escaping, changing, denying, repressing, acting out, or discharging. This habit of mind is ego. If this habit is recognized and set free, then where is ego? When you are not preoccupied and distracted by thoughts of escaping or clinging, seeing is clear. Seeing clearly is the inherent nature of consciousness.

Egoic habits of mind have been passed from generation to generation for millions of years. Strategies of escape or defense nourish the momentum of conditioned existence.

In the willingness to experience what has not been experienced, the core of all internal and external phenomena is revealed, and the momentum of conditioning is stopped.

Expose and release the lie of ego. All of our lives are conditioned toward complexity, yet release is absolutely simple.

Every emotion, sensation, or energy faced purely and simply reveals eternal Self.

• • •

I'm troubled because the doctors say I must work with them or I'll die.

Are you ready to die?

I don't think that would be as bad as mucking around with doctors.

I have nothing against medical procedures or medicine. What I am *for* is you facing your death. Not just because someone has now spoken of the possibility of death to you, but because every body will die at some point.

There is no lasting clarity before death has been faced. Before the meeting with death, countless hours are spent ignoring, fearing, chasing, wallowing in, or running from this thing we call death. Every decision and every choice is based on some kind of mental relationship with death. When the mind is kept busy running from, worrying about, thinking about, or denying thoughts about death, what is eternal is overlooked. Surrender the relationship with mind, and have a meeting with death.

Let me stress that surrender has nothing to do with either tending the body or not tending it. The decision to care for the body is not muddied with needs and hopes and expectations once death has been met.

When Ramana was a sixteen year old boy, he experienced a fear of death. Rather than run to his mother, or to the doctors, he lay down on the floor and faced it fully; not just intellectually, but fully and completely. He allowed himself to experience directly what it is that actually dies. From a true meeting, great awakening occurs. In finally facing death fully, completely, there is recognition of Life. Life that is not born, and therefore not subject to death.

Most people spend their lives ignoring the reality of the death of the body, and then they are quite surprised when it is their body's turn. Ninety-year old people are still surprised. It is part of the education of our culture that death is pretended to be something separate from life. In our culture, death usually takes place in the back room. Bring the specter of death into the front room. Welcome death to satsang.

What a gift the prognosis of death is. The most feared event is announced. The announcement is your invitation to direct experience.

Everyone's body has a prognosis of death. What an attention-getter. What a way to draw attention to what does not die.

• • •

When I met you the very first time, I was so touched by what you said. At home afterwards, I felt like everything was breaking and burning.

Wonderful.

Yes, but it's scary.

Yes, it is not casual. It is not trivial. The whole mental house of cards is shaken.

Then I tried to accept it, to meet it, and it was very difficult because it's so scary.

Now stop trying anything. Let it be scary.

Then the fear arises that I cannot manage my life.

Yes, I know this fear. You fear that you will not be able to manage your life, or even that you will not survive. Those fears are all the fear *of* something. The fear of death, the fear of homelessness, the fear of irresponsibility. Fear *of* goes on and on. Approach fear itself. As long as you stay with fear *of* something, you are hovering on the perimeter. Discover in truth, what is fear?
Are you aware of this fear now?

Yes.

Leaving all speculations behind, report to me from the core of it.

It's difficult.

In the core of fear, where is difficulty?
Where is fear?

136

Something that I learned.

Well, that's true, but I want your report to be deeper than an analysis. In the midst of this something that you have learned to name fear, what is found?

It is a fear of not existing.

Ah, ha! The primary fear is the possibility of nonexistence.

Effortlessly fall into and *be* the fear of nonexistence. Any mental effort is the scramble to try to escape nonexistence.

Release any effort to reject the fear. Let go of all struggle to not be touched by that fear, and meet nonexistence.

I appreciate that it is a colossal fear. In your willingness to meet this colossus directly, the truth is discovered.

Notice if you are telling yourself a story, or even just aimlessly talking to yourself. If so, stop. Allow the mind to be open.

Now I feel a lot of body sensations.

Let them be. They mean nothing. Let sensations, energy, phenomena of all kind, be.

See how easy it is?

Now where is fear?

No where!

Yes. Now you know the truth of ease, and the truth of difficulty. Difficulty arises when you try to escape the experience of something. Easy is present when you are willing to stop and meet whatever has been haunting you.

When you finally, completely face fear itself, it is nowhere to be found. Fear can never survive total meeting with consciousness.

• • •

The closer I come to being in labor, to giving birth, the more I fear death.

Open to the fear of death today, right now. Don't continue the habitual tendency to contract the mind.

Right now is the time. The fear of death is deep in the psyche. When it arises to the surface, there is usually the impulse to either overcome it or to get away from it. Now you hear the suggestion to open. For this opening, all the stories about death must close. Open to the fear of death.

It doesn't seem scary if I open to it.

That's right.

Certainly death is an extremely powerful event, as is birth. Whatever appears to be born, dies. Whatever appears, disappears. Whether it is flesh, idea, thought, emotion, or state.

What is not born cannot die. Death is not the end of life. Death is not the polar opposite of life. Birth and death are opposites. Life is the constant. Life is the presence that both birth and death appear in.

Be willing to die before the flesh dies. Give up the struggle against the fear of death. When you face fear of death, you discover it to be a nonexistent guardian to the gates of realization. You do not need to overcome what is nonexistent.

Usually fear is transmitted through the womb, as well as anguish, desire, hope, failure, and success. When you are willing to meet fear, the realization of what is true is transmitted from being to being. You will have transmitted an extraordinary secret of life through the womb.

• • •

I've been going through a lot of loss lately. Today I thought I was going to lose my life. The fear of death came up, and I'm wondering how to address that fear.

Invite the fear back. Right now as you sit here— invite it to show its face in the light of satsang.

I can't seem to get it to come.

Yes, this is the secret.

Fear is powerful only when you are trying to escape it. Turn to fear and say, "Yes, come now. I am ready." You will see how fearful fear is. It is not to be found.

Through past generations, your ancestors have run from fear. Finally, down the line, one of you awakens and says, "Okay, I'm ready to see. Where are you, fear?" Direct experience goes against the momentum of conditioned existence.

Look for fear and tell me, what is present? Call it in more strongly. If fear of death shows up at satsang, it is ready to be liberated. If it is not ready to be liberated, it runs as far from you as it can.

Welcome all to satsang. This meeting called satsang is not different from simple willingness to be. Just be.

Now you know the secret of fear, both because you have spent so much time running from it, and more importantly, because you have stopped to face it. Now fear is a useful vehicle to discover the divine secret.

Keep the invitation open. The minute you begin to close your mind some fear from back in time may appear to chase you. Open the door and where can it be found?

• • •

I'm not sure what to do about fearing death for my children. My son just wrote me, and he is in a very dangerous place.

Your fear is not about your child's death. It is about your own death. Until the nature of your own death is recognized, you will project your fear onto others.

Every body is in a dangerous situation at every moment. The body is a walking time bomb. At any moment it could cease to be. Your body and your children's bodies will one day cease to exist. To become involved in your children's death before you meet your own is a distraction that serves only in the continuance of fear.

I understand the pull on you, but facing your own death is all you can do. And, in fact, it is enough. If your children have stirred up this fear of death, very good. Bow to them. Stirring up what hasn't been faced is one of the great attributes of children.

It is impossible to know that a child will live from day one on. If you are distracted by the thought of that, you overlook meeting what has been stirred up. Stop using your thoughts to delay meeting any emotion that appears from this stirring. Take five seconds to turn and face what you have run from.

Your children will be much happier if you face your own death. They will receive a transmission from you of the willingness to meet death fully. And when you speak to them about anything, you will speak from that realization.

He also worries about death.

He learned to worry from you. The same way he learned his name, or his first word. The fear of death is contagious. You must stop the contagion. Facing death is the medicine to cure the disease. If the disease is exposed to the medicine, the disease cannot survive.

But he can be stabbed. He can be beat up.

Yes, of course. Always. The difference meeting death makes is in the quality and experience of life. Are you wandering around looking for the potential stabbing or imagining the potential stabbing while fantasizing the loneliness? This is the way most people spend their lives, isn't it?

He says he hears gunfire in his neighborhood, and it's not his imagination.

141

Death is in every neighborhood. Do you think death is located only in particular neighborhoods just because it is obvious there? Death is in every house.

I am not speaking of the outer circumstances of his life. I am speaking of the inner circumstances of your life. Your life right now. Your own death.

You have learned the horror of death. You have seen pictures of it, you have read books about it. You have thought about it, and now you are imagining your child in that horror. This is a nightmare. Wake up in this nightmare.

You cannot control death. You can move to the biggest house with the biggest security fence, and still you cannot control death. You need only read the newspapers to see that this is so. Violence is the by-product of a fearful, violent society. There is no help for a society running from fear.

Running from fear leads to isolation and separation. The desperate attempt to control the enormous fear of death fosters more fear, more isolation, and more violence.

It must begin with you. The whole world is waiting for you. I am serious. I am speaking to everyone. It is no good to wait for someone else to awaken, so that then all will be taken care of. It is you the world is waiting for. Not just for your children, but for all children, all neighborhoods everywhere. It is up to you. *You* must awaken and discover directly what has never been born and therefore cannot die. This is the real heritage for children. Anything else is just passing on further conditioning based on fear.

• • •

I have a question about the mind and the body. I often have this tiredness that affects my everyday life, and I was wondering about the power of the mind to heal.

The power of mind is enormous and can be used to support either sickness or health. I suggest you only accept the true healing. The only true refuge. All the rest is playing with feelings of personal power.

Many people seek personal power because there is a promise of security. Then one day the body dies. I suggest you discover what is beyond healing the body.

Take care of your body, even love your body. Feed it properly, exercise it properly, give it proper rest. If it is sick, give it medicine; but don't think that it is who you are. If you think the body is who you are, it will never satisfy you. This misidentification and the dissatisfaction that follows it is the larger sickness.

Generally, when I speak about illness, I am addressing psychological illness. I define psychological sickness as the notion that you are separate from the source of fulfillment, or that you need something else to make you happy. This sickness is epidemic.

If you believe "*I* am sick," then there is suffering and the attempt to escape suffering. Stop all attempts to escape and ask yourself, *Who is sick?*

Be willing to discover the truth behind your sense of lack of fulfillment. Be willing to receive the revelation of that which is always whole; your own Self.

One of the clarifying experiences of an aging body is the recognition that death of the form really happens. It is not abstract. The body does return to dust.

Some bodies will have more sickness than other bodies. Some plants grow stronger than others. This is simply the nature of form. If you cease seeking fulfillment through the body, there is no problem. There may be physical discomfort, but discomfort does not mean anything about the source of fulfillment. The truth is that who you truly and always are, is already complete.

Face whatever it is that you imagine separates you from fulfillment, rather than continually trying to outrun some physical or psychological sickness.

First face the psychological lie that you are incomplete, that you are not good enough. Face this directly, rather than trying to get complete, or become enlightened, or be worth something. Face incompleteness directly, and discover immediately what is true.

The extraordinary, good news is revealed at the core of every fear, as well as at the core of every other emotion. With exquisite irony, when you stop expecting the body and its condition to lead you to fulfillment, you can see clearly what your particular body actually needs and provide it.

• • •

Recently I had the experience of being in an MRI machine. I could not move, and I had a panic attack. I thought I was going to die, and there was a loss of control that I couldn't let go into. Can you help?

There may be great fear of losing control, but, in fact, each night before you drop into deep sleep you have to lose all control. It is impossible to go into deep sleep without

losing control. If you are still attempting to control anything, you won't sleep, or your sleep will be very light and
filled with dreams.

As you give up control, the definition of who you are is
released. With the death of definition, all thoughts of what
you can and cannot do naturally also die. Since there is no
thought of you, there are no thoughts of what can or cannot
be borne, what can be done or cannot be done. Thoughts of
what should have been, or might have been are all finished,
all with simply giving up the illusion of control.

I am not suggesting that you lose control of bodily functions or lose control of thoughts or lose control of emotions.
You have lost control of these many times and loss of control of these has not revealed the peace you crave. These
functions are naturally, effortlessly controlled in surrendering to life.

I understand the great fear that if you give up control,
you might become like a vegetable, or a madman, or something horrible. But you are like a madman in your attempt
to keep control over what cannot be controlled. Life cannot
be controlled.

At a certain stage of maturity, you recognize you have
no control over life. Life is the true satguru. However you
may try you will never be able to control a true teacher, a
true satguru, life. When you recognize life, the satguru, as
the uncontrollable teacher, the concept of control is hum-
bled. In this humbling, life then lives its life form in fulfillment.

I am not suggesting you give up control to somebody. I
am saying surrender your idea of who you are, and all defi-

145

nitions of who you are. These ideas are all just some futile attempt to control Life.

· · ·

If this body, this form, is illusion and not the true Self, it almost seems like a cosmic joke. Why aren't we just this source?

You are.

Limitlessness has no problem with form. Why limit Self to either form or formlessness? Do you think we should be limited to no jokes? Do you think God is not playful?

Well, I guess I don't mind a joke unless it's played on me!

The best joke is the one played on oneself. That joke destroys any idea of self-importance.

If you were two or three or even ten years old, maybe I would not speak to you like this; but now you are long past your time of maturity, so get the joke. Enjoy the joke. The joke itself destroys the knot of identification. Self-righteousness and self-importance are ego-righteousness and ego-importance. Recognizing the joke is the medicine for the disease of egoic importance.

It is a beautiful joke. A joke with uncountable levels and permutations, tears and laughter, longing and beauty, and silence. A divine joke. Not a paltry joke that can be read in a book. It is the most mysterious, far-reaching, never-ending joke. This is Leela's joke.

· · ·

It's as though my body is physically struggling with this. My heart is beating very, very fast. The fear grows, and I open to the fear. I realize it is really the fear of losing this body.

The primal identification, the primal struggle, the primal fear is that without your body, you do not exist. You believe that your body is where you exist and is the proof of your existence. This fear must be met. This is the purpose of satsang.

Relax and allow the fear to be. There may be great shaking. There may be energy released. There may be sweating. There may be tears. There may be the impulse to bolt, the impulse to cover one's face. All of this is normal, given the deep conditioning of identification with the body.

Relax. The fear is a good sign. If people tell me they never have fear, I realize they probably have not touched this primal fear.

The gift from Ramana instructs you to lie down and see, *Who dies?*

Self-inquiry is not intellectual inquiry. It is of the deepest order. It is the great good luck of this human incarnation that there is the capacity to ask a question of such depth, to actually question death itself.

You are the source, untouched by birth or death. You are that pure, boundless, unborn consciousness— giving birth to all bodies, and reclaiming all bodies in death. You have nothing to fear! Take a moment to die, and you can see clearly, obviously, what dies and what is eternal Self. Then your body, for as long as it may exist, is no problem. Even though it may have problems, it is no problem.

147

True Meaning of Vigilance

Is it essential to maintain vigilance? Can you give us some guidelines?

Vigilance is essential. The problem with the word vigilance is that it is misunderstood to mean an imposition of strenuous discipline. Vigilance is discipline, but it is the discipline of surrender.

If there is the slightest pulling of attention from what is free, from what is boundless and endless, suffering is experienced. When suffering is experienced, the habitual tendency of mind arises to then deny truth. By being vigilant, the capacity of thought to deny truth is acknowledged and seen through.

If effort is used for the maintenance of vigilance, sooner or later there is exhaustion. However, if you relax your mind, your individual mind-stream is already naturally aligned with the ocean of pure awareness. Then alertness, vigilance, surrender, and discipline are all effortless.

Being still reveals non-identified awareness that is Self-aware intelligence. If the impulse to effort appears— and it may, because efforting is a strong tendency—recognize that this very effort assumes that you are not that awareness. Check, has pure awareness moved? In truth, is there any separation between you and pure awareness?

Self-inquiry is vigilance. If in any moment you feel pulled towards identification with suffering, ask the question, *Who is suffering?*

The belief, *I am not That,* and the resulting suffering must be faced. Direct experience is Self-inquiry. *Who* is not That? *Who is suffering?* In Self-inquiry, one uncovers Self-denial through fabrication of thought. Belief in fabrication as reality leads to suffering. In the moment of directly experiencing the fabrication, the lie is exposed and annihilated. Seeing is vigilance.

What do I do when I am totally hooked into the drama that is going on?

Drop the story instantly. Instantly! To be hooked you must be feeding the storyline with more commentary or searching for release through a different storyline. Drama might appear from past feedings, but it cannot continue without present feeding.

Be very aware of how you maintain past, present, and future. Vigilance breaks the imaginary bonds called "me" and "my drama."

Do you always have a choice, in any moment, to not keep feeding energy to the drama that's happening?

Yes, you always have the choice.

My suggestion is that you direct all power of choice toward recognizing the truth of who you are in every moment. Surrender the power of choice to deny truth. Give it up. Declare that you will no longer choose to believe that you are separate from truth itself, even in suffering, in drama, in grief, in adverse circumstances of all kinds.

The usual choice is to overlook pure, radiant awareness. Surrender that choice on the altar of truth. You may be tested, but if you have really given up the choice to deny truth, you will not be tempted.

Declare yourself married to truth, and be faithful regardless of which old lovers come to ask you to play. Declare that you have chosen truth, and nothing can separate you from that. Old lovers may appear. Let them appear. If they are not entertained, they disappear.

Few people have the courage for this divine marriage because it is imagined that pleasure comes from playing around with old habits. Playing around is normal in a certain stage of immaturity. In maturity, one realizes there has been enough playing around. There has been enough going from this thing to that thing.

In silence, the true Beloved reveals itself. There then is the possibility of choosing the Beloved and giving up all other choices, all others.

This is the potential. Satsang is the wedding invitation. Recognize that the Beloved is here. Regardless of busyness, regardless of pain, regardless of pleasure, it is here. It has been waiting patiently, lovingly, for you to finish your playing around.

Love of truth is mature love, but if you are fixated on adolescent fantasies, it can seem terrifying. It is feared that in mature love something will be lost. Yes. And that loss is the gain of realization.

Choosing truth demands giving up flirting with egocentric arrogance and egocentric Self-denial. Be willing to give up both egocentric pleasure and egocentric pain for the Beloved, and then tell me what you have given up.

• • •

I can discover freedom in silence, but to discover it in action is difficult.

The distinction you make between silence and action is artificial. Silence does not go anywhere when action appears. There is no action separate from silence.

Have you found the boundary of silence?

The boundary is that as soon as I find myself in activity and thoughts and the mind, then I'm lost.

What does *I am lost* mean?

Days or weeks can go by before I notice the silence again.

In these days and weeks, does awareness go anywhere?

The awareness was not aware of itself.

But it was aware?

There was awareness in every moment.

There is awareness in every moment. Is awareness separate from silence?

I've never looked at that.

Well, look. There is always more to see.

Events happen in awareness. Your individual mindstream may be consciously aware of an event or subconsciously aware. Just in this moment, turn your individual mind-stream toward that ocean of awareness that is aware of your individual mind-stream as an event.

Conscious and subconscious awareness dissolve in the ocean of pure awareness. Events remembered and events forgotten dissolve here. Here you are– purely *I*.

I am lost. *I* am found. *I* am in meditation. *I* am at work. *I* am having a good time. *I* am having a bad time. *I* am ignorant. *I* am enlightened. There is still *I*, just *I*. The true *I* does not go anywhere.

So, focus on the I in every moment?

Focus on the *I* right now, and tell me, what do you find?

There is only awareness.

Thank you. Do you see?

Yes!

Yes. It is wonderful that you recognize this in an instant in satsang. This is the halfway point. To complete your journey, begin to explore; does awareness go anywhere? Is true *I* ever lost?

When you think, *I am lost,* check. Who has gone? Has awareness gone anywhere? Experience of lostness has appeared in awareness, but has awareness been affected?

Recognize directly what is always present and cannot be other than present. Then stop looking for particular states to confirm that.

Once you have experienced this confirmation directly, every state is a reconfirmation. Experience of loss, bliss, sadness, good events, bad events, are all recognized to appear in awareness. Finally, totality of experience is the reconfirmation, *I am That. I AM*. Before and after any thought of what I am or how I am or where I am, *I AM*.

• • •

Following an instant of realizing pure silent awareness, there is a great rush of many physiological and emotional effects. The tendency is to become attached to these by-products. When the by-products are finished, or change, or transform, the thought may arise, *Oh, I lost myself.* Do you hear the absurdity of this thought? Where can you go? Only *thoughts* of you go.

Events come and go. Thoughts come and go. Moods come and go. Good times come and go. Bad times come and go. Awareness is always present. You are awareness.

Awareness, your own Self, is vast beyond measure, and has no problem with anything appearing or disappearing in it. Everything is included.

Even your past, which seemed to be pulling you away from silence, is a confirmation of eternal, silent presence of awareness. Without awareness, how can imagination of past appear? See for yourself.

In every moment?

Yes, in every moment. Now we are speaking of vigilance!

• • •

What is enlightenment? Is it, every single moment, keeping the awareness on awareness?

Enlightenment is a word which points to the recognition of totality as Self. Unfortunately, the word enlightenment has become conceptualized as the experiential by-product that results from that recognition. True enlightenment is not limited to any state of mind.

True enlightenment recognizes that which is present before, during, and after any notion of enlightenment. That which is unaffected by either the state of enlightenment or the state of unenlightenment.

• • •

I had an image of climbing a ladder, and it seemed that every rung of the ladder was a realization or an accomplishment. Then all of a sudden the ladder turned into a greased pole. At first it felt like I was falling down and backwards. Now, there's just no direction to it at all, and it's a delightful ride.

The first step is in giving up your defeats. Give up your hell, your insanity, your personal samsara. Next, give up your victories, your accomplishments, your self-importance. Really fall. Free fall.

Give up the old ladder of accomplishments. Whatever is acquired must be defended. This defense fraudulently uses the name of vigilance. Defending is not vigilance. Vigilance is the willingness to free fall through all illusion.

The moment the identification, *I am somebody*, arises, directly inquire into its reality. Then falling is not falling. In direct self-inquiry, rising and falling are not separate. In and out; no separation. Truth and you; no separation. Life and you; no separation.

• • •

I notice when my mind is quiet, it is very easy to be aware of myself, and see what arises and not touch it. But throughout the day I forget, and I have to keep myself coming back to vigilance. I feel that vigilance takes effort.

The effort follows the misunderstanding that vigilance means to capture some particular state. The idea that there is some particular state that identifies you, as Self, is spiritual conditioning. Stop all attempts to capture.

Do not make vigilance an exercise. Be vigilant by surrendering all effort to define yourself according to mental or emotional states.

Effort is not needed to *be*. If you trust being, and begin to explore into being, *as being*, then can you find any activity separate from your Self?

Vigilance is attention. Attention gets its attentiveness from pure awareness, which is who you are. Self-definition only keeps you fixated on waves while yearning to find the deep. The ocean has no problem with waves. Never for a moment does the ocean imagine the waves as separate from itself. Never for a moment does the ocean imagine its depths as separate from itself. Never for a moment does the ocean imagine there is any separation between wave and depth.

Be the ocean. This is vigilance.

You Are That!

You will never be satisfied until you realize who you are. The time is now.

• • •

I was having a conversation with a supposedly very learned man and he said, "Just like the clouds that go in front of the sun have to be removed . . ." How do I remove the clouds that obstruct realization?

Clouds that go in front of the sun have to be removed only if you imagine that you are not the sun. If you are the sun, what can it matter that clouds pass by? Do they block your own light from yourself? If your point of view is that you are separate from the light, then anything that appears has the potential to come between you and that light. Recognize that the core of your being radiates light. What can separate you from that?

You are even more than the sun. You are the sky. By *sky*, I don't mean the upper atmosphere of our planet. Here the word "sky" refers to endless, limitless, spacious consciousness. The power that gives rise to clouds and the power that gives rise to dissipation of clouds is in the sky. This power cannot be imagined. It is too big to be thought. The sky of consciousness is inclusive of all, blocked by nothing.

What are clouds and what is sun in consciousness?

Perceived images. You are the sky. The sun is an image that arises in you. The image of light exists in the sky of consciousness. The sky is infinitely larger than any image.

In your mind you may imagine that consciousness or God or Truth or sky is up there somewhere. But really, where does it begin? Where does it end? When is it ever absent? Even if you close yourself into a closet, is the sky of consciousness absent? No, it is never absent.

Clouds are born in you and die in you. If you begin to identify yourself with phenomena, such as clouds, there is unnecessary suffering. If you identify yourself with the cloud called the body, there is the experience of separation from the eternal sky of consciousness.

The true sky is endless. It is both forever beyond and immediately present. It goes forever. It is forever here. Different realms, different universes, and different solar systems, yes, but all exist within the sky of consciousness. In true identification, you recognize yourself as that. Recognize yourself truly, and there is no problem with any cloud, or sunset, or even eclipse. Different climatic events are just phenomena. Atmospheric weather, emotional weather, and mental weather do not affect the sky of consciousness.

Early astronomy once imagined that the sun and planets revolved around the Earth. This type of primitive thinking is still within our psyche. Misidentification must be realized to be old thinking that is useless and must now be discarded.

This philosophy of the sky as Self is easy to talk, but it is hard to realize.

You are partially right. It is easy to talk, but it is even easier to realize. Ease is the secret. Books and teachers and parents and friends and enemies have told you, "It is hard, it is difficult." Now the cloud, *It is difficult*, has become a part of your primitive belief system. You walk around thinking, *Awakening is hard, realization is difficult.*

With the thought of difficulty, awakening is experienced as hard, realization is experienced as difficult. I am telling you that awakening is inherently easy. You are already that which you are seeking in awakening. Put aside your commentary and see.

Is it easy to stay in that state of mind all the time?

No state of mind is present all the time. States of mind are like clouds, appearing and disappearing.

Even that feeling you were talking about?

Feelings come and go. You are that sky that feelings and states come and go in. You are That!

It is not a question of if you *feel* you are that, then you are that. You are that, whatever the feeling

What about life?

Life is that! You *are* life!

So, all is Self-realization?

All is Self. There is no separation anywhere.

Suffering comes while imagining separation from Self. Fear arises around whatever it is you imagine you are separate from. You wonder, *Is this enemy or is this friend?* Fear based relating is very ancient. Dogs and pigs and even protoplasm in a petri dish relate in protective, fear-based ways. Somehow, with a human birth, there is a gateway through that fear.

The gateway is the call and the promise of all who have awakened. This is the good news of the Buddha, the good news of Christ, the good news of Mohammed; *Consciousness is one, I and God are one, Allah is one.* Whoever awakens declares the possibility of realizing *You Are That Oneness.*

• • •

What you are telling me is very familiar.

I am telling you what you already know.

Now trust what you know beyond what has been told to you. Trust deeper than what you have read or believed or followed.

• • •

I feel very serious about this, and it also makes me fall into desperateness.

Why not fall into seriousness?

I feel it is so important.

It is important. It is the most important, and you must be absolutely serious. However, if by serious you mean rigid, then your seriousness is absurd.

I think the rigidity is the problem.

True seriousness is resolve. True resolve must be immovable. Resolve is serious sometimes, and light-hearted and joyful at other times. Resolve uses all faces.

The tide of conditioning, temptation, and Self-doubt is very large, isn't it?

Oh, yes!

Without serious resolve, satsang will be just another experience in your mental bundle of experiences. I applaud your resolve. I bow to your resolve.

You must strap yourself to this resolve, to this Bodhi Tree, to this mountain peak, to this cave, and not be moved.

There will be tests of your resolve. Tests reveal the depth of resolve. Let the whole world come to try and move you, including God itself. Be immovable.

Whenever I feel my resolve isn't great enough, I get angry with myself, and I want to let that anger go.

You do not have to let go of anger. Just keep full attention on the truth of who you are. Anger may arise. All emotions and states arise and pass. If you fix attention on the story of anger, then you are back into the old sordid relationship with it, and attention is pulled from the truth of who you are.

Many tendencies arise to be burned. In resolve, if you have one tendency left or thirty-five million tendencies, it does not matter, because that is not where your attention is.

Let whatever arises, arise. In letting it arise, you let it go. It is only when you pull your attention away from the truth of who you are that you get into the story of what should or should not arise.

Be prepared for everything to arise. Be prepared for nothing to arise. It is the same, really, and this is the great secret.

Enormous feelings of suffering may arise. In the moment, you are willing for everything to arise while your attention is firmly, resolutely, attached to that in which all arises, suffering cannot continue.

If you call some state or emotion or event suffering, call it conscious suffering, and as awareness itself, meet suffering. Running from suffering is samsara. In your willingness to directly experience whatever arises, then suffering is not suffering. Samsara is not samsara.

Jesus is reported as having said, "If you know how to suffer, you do not suffer."

How to suffer? By willingly, completely, and unsentimentally asking, "Who is suffering?"

• • •

This week at massage school when I was being worked on, I had a feeling of going into a different space where it was really happy and blissful, but there was nothing there.

Yes!

My teacher kept trying to lead me back.

Leading you back to known reality is the normal teaching. Luckily you are not a normal student.

I looked around at the surroundings, and it felt like I had been beamed somewhere. Then I ran into confusion as to why I'm even in a body. Why can't I just be in that other place all the time?

You are. Your body is in that all the time. Your body is never separate from that.

But it is.

No, it's not.

Are they both just as real as one another?

There is that which is permanently real, and there are experiences in That which seem real, look real, and feel real, but are limited in duration. Your body is an example of limited, impermanent experience. In satsang, the word *real* refers to what is permanently present, not what appears real and then disappears.

People sometimes do not want the body to continue. People sometimes want the body to continue forever. Both desires reflect the same misidentification. Some get the idea to get rid of the body to return to the final truth. You must recognize that truth is here now. It is the animating force of all bodies, and it exists independently of any body. Only if the body is either worshipped or reviled is it a problem. In either worshipping or reviling what is limited, the limitless source is overlooked.

So, why do bodies feel so separate from one another?

They feel separate because they appear to be separate, and we are trained to accept our perceptions as reality. There is deep conditioning that you are a particular body. For an instant, there is the glimpse of freedom with no body present. This glimpse is the cut in the knot of misidentification.

Directly experience the body, and you will see. At its core, at the core of every cell, at the core of every phenomena, is that limitlessness which is bound by no body.

• • •

Can you speak further on a word you've touched on at other satsangs, "unborn"?

When you own nothing—not your body, not your name, not your history, not your fear, not your courage, not your conclusions—then you recognize yourself to be that which is forever unborn. Even deeper than unborn; *that which is forever unconceived.*

The moment that conception arises, stop. What is before that? Purity before and beyond all conception is the truth of who you are. This purity does not go away during conception or after conception. It is immovable. It is untouched by anything conceived.

What is unborn and unconceived has nowhere to go. In this moment, discover within yourself that peace which has nowhere to go. It is forever unborn, and yet all that is born is born of it.

• • •

Satsang is not limited to something read or heard. Satsang is the potential context for every moment of your whole life.

You are not separate from any awakening that has ever occurred. You are not separate from Buddha's awakening, Christ's awakening, Ramana's awakening, Poonjaji's awakening, or any other awakening. It is the same awakening. The same Self awakening to Itself, crossing all lines of religion and culture, boundaries and horizons. Crossing all lines of perceived differences and separation. Recognizing Itself totally and without limit. Each one has some exquisite role to play, an unknown, mysterious role. The possibility in satsang is to be inspired to play that role fully. To play a role fully, recognize that any role is just a role, and that who you truly are is beyond all roles.

If you end mental fixation on personal problems, awakening of Self to Itself is served. Your life is then naturally used to facilitate the awakening of all being. Service to awakening is discovered to be the deepest bliss.

• • •

Now is the time to recognize the core of peace that exists within yourself. You are That!

Yes, now is the time.

The Gangaji Foundation
& Satsang Press

The Gangaji Foundation serves the truth of universal consciousness and the potential for individual and collective recognition of peace, inherent in the core of all being. It is the mission of the Gangaji Foundation to forthrightly and respectfully present to as many people as possible the teaching and transmission of Gangaji in the lineage of Sri Ramana Maharshi and Sri H.W.L. Poonjaji.

For information on books, audio and video tapes of Ramana Maharshi, Poonjaji (Papaji), and Gangaji, or subscription information for the *Satsang with Gangaji* newsletter, please contact:

Satsang Press
4855 Riverbend Road
Boulder, CO 80301

Phone: (303) 415-1000
Fax: (303) 449-6633

For information on books, audio and video tapes of Poonjaji (Papaji), please contact:

The Avadhuta Foundation
2888 Bluff Street Ste. 390
Boulder, CO 80301

For information on Gangaji satsang and retreat schedules, Gangaji video showings, and the Gangaji Foundation, please contact:

The Gangaji Foundation
4855 Riverbend Road
Boulder, CO 80301

Phone: (303) 449-6325
Fax: (303) 449-6633

The Gangaji Foundation is a non-profit organization, supported primarily by donations.